# MY EIGHTY YEARS
# IN PENTECOST

*To Marilyn:*

*May my story enrich yours!*

# MY EIGHTY YEARS
# IN PENTECOST

*Charles T. Crabtree*

## CHARLES T. CRABTREE

XULON PRESS

Xulon Press
2301 Lucien Way #415
Maitland, FL 32751
407.339.4217
www.xulonpress.com

Printed in the United States of America.

ISBN-13: 978-1-54565-541-2

# Table of Contents

# FOREWORD

**It should not surprise anyone to learn that book** publishers are rarely interested in printing and selling biographies and especially autobiographies. Only the lives and achievements of very famous people would motivate enough buyers to make such a project financially feasible. So why, you may ask, did you write the book "My Eighty Years In Pentecost"?

My original purpose in writing my autobiography was to document my story for my family and their descendants. I planned to simply print a few copies on a computer. However, as the story began to unfold I realized many of my friends and possibly a larger audience of people in the Pentecostal world might find my life experience not only interesting but helpful.

Very few people, if any, were born into the home of an independent Pentecostal pastor who received the baptism in the Holy Spirit under the ministry of such a famous evangelist Aimee Simple McPherson in a tent revival meeting in Northern Maine.

It would be my privilege to become an Assemblies of God evangelist, pastor, denominational executive and Bible college president.

During my ministerial training I was taught history and doctrine of the Assemblies of God by J. Roswell Flower who was a founding member and official delegate to the first General Council of the Assemblies of God held in Hot Springs, Arkansas, in 1914.

Through the years I have met many Pentecostal world leaders, preaching as a guest in several denominations in the United States and around the world and in hundreds of Assemblies of God churches.

It is my prayer that my story will be used of God to inspire and educate many future Pentecostal leaders.

# CHAPTER 1

I was born on October 20, 1937, in a church which would prove to be most appropriate in light of my future career. The church, located in Halifax, Nova Scotia, was pastored by my father, Clifford Alden Crabtree. The parsonage was housed on the second floor of the church where I chose to make my grand entrance into the world.

They tell me I arrived very early in the morning before the doctor could get there. In those days it was almost unheard of for babies to be born in hospitals because of the cost. My mother did have a woman who lived close by who served as a midwife to assist in my birth until the doctor could take over.

My first "sermon" was delivered with a loud cry and caused a great stir which woke up my five-year-old brother, David, who upon being told by my father he had a new baby brother proceeded to jump up and down in his bed and yell, "Let's call him Little Charlie." My four-year-old sister, Hazel, slept through the whole event which means I was not worth losing sleep over. That is one of the reasons I started life with a terrible inferiority complex.

My name is Charles Talmage. There are several accounts of why they decided to settle on such a distinguished title. Of course, my brother's initial input was in the mix. (I am glad my first name was not Little and my second Charlie). The doctor who finally arrived was a fan of Charles Lindbergh; and since the whole world was celebrating the tenth anniversary of his amazing feat and I had "flown in and landed" before he got there, he thought Charles would be a good name for me. My father had a brother the family called "Uncle Tal" who had died in the Klondike, so some of the family wanted me to be named in his honor. The account I liked best was my mother's. She claimed she wanted me to be named after two famous preachers she enjoyed reading: Charles Spurgeon and T. Dewitt Talmage. Since I was very close to my mother starting at birth, I have chosen to accept her explanation of my name.

In no way do I want to give you the opinion I am especially smart, but I did arrange to get special treatment from birth. When the doctor examined me, he discovered a heart murmur which he said was quite common with newborns at the time. He told my folks it was not serious but he wanted them to do everything they could to keep me from crying too hard for the first few months of my life. Was that not a brilliant move on my part? I did grow out of the heart murmur, but I did not let my folks know for a long time.

My father's story is quite unique. He was born in 1903 in Easton, Maine, which was, at the time, a "rock farm" in Aroostook County, Maine, meaning there was very little tillable land to grow potatoes which was about the only crop produced in the county. Rocks were in great supply.

My dad was the firstborn son of a family of 13 which meant he had to work alongside his father from an early age in order to help keep food on the table. In reality, he had no childhood. During the winter months, he was able to go to a one-room school house about a mile from his home, leaving after early chores and returning near dusk to do evening chores. In the summer, he worked approx-imately 14 hours a day and left school after the eighth grade. He told me that one day after he had been working especially hard, he told his dad in total frustration, "You and Mom have got to stop having kids; we have too many already!" to which his dad turned to him with a twinkle in his eye and asked, "Well, Cliff, which ones should we send back?" He had no answer for that.

In his late teens, my dad's world changed. In 1918 the famous woman preacher, Aimee Semple McPherson, held a tent meeting about two miles from Dad's home. It was probably the greatest event in the history of that county. One night, my father responded to the altar appeal and with deep conviction gave his heart to the Lord. He told me two things happened almost immediately. He received the gift of the Holy Spirit with the initial physical evidence of speaking in tongues; and while praising God in his new tongue, Mrs. McPherson came over to him, laid her hands on his head, and said, "God, I pray you will make this young man a mighty preacher of the New Testament." From that moment, my dad was an "incur-able" Pentecostal and knew his destiny was to preach the gospel for the rest of his life. It not only changed him but also scores of others who lived in the county. Many became Pentecostal believers.

Looking back, the visit of Amie Semple McPherson to Aroostook County and the subsequent baptism of the Holy Spirit my father received would, in reality, be the reason for my 80 years of growing up and ministering in the world of Pentecostalism. In order to understand my story, it is absolutely necessary to understand the context of the very misunderstood culture into which I was born and raised, beginning with the background of my parents' spiritual journeys.

The reason I first bring focus to the life and ministry of Amie Semple McPherson is because of the powerful influence she had on my father. She was born and raised in Ontario, Canada, in a Methodist/Salvation Army home. At a very early age, she received the Pentecostal experience and felt the call of God to be an evangelist. She married Robert Semple who died a little over two years later. She then married Harold McPherson whom she quietly divorced a few years later. It was after that marriage was dissolved she preached the revival in Aroostook County during which she prayed for my father. She would go on to become one of the most popular Pentecostal preachers in American history. She founded and built the Angelus Temple seating 5,300 people. She claimed God gave her the design for the building which included the largest unsupported dome up to that time anywhere in the United States. She consistently packed out the Temple and, being a born actress, did many illustrated sermons. One the most notable called for her to ride to the platform on a ramp from the outside on a motorcycle. She also founded the International Church of the Foursquare denomination. The mystery of her disappearance for several days after swimming in the Pacific Ocean was never truly solved; but in spite of her controversial life, she remained popular to the end of her life at age 54. At her death the Los Angeles police estimated over 150,000 people lined the streets to view her funeral cortege to her final resting place in Forest Lawn. I was only seven when she died, but I can still remember my father crying, one of the few times I had ever seen him do so, when he received the news of her passing.

At the time of my father's baptism, Pentecostal denominations were unknown or in their infant stages. The only thing that held Pentecostals together was the experience of speaking in tongues. Most of them were very suspicious of denominations because many of them viewed the baptism of the Holy Spirit as delivering them from man-made organizations. Before the revival with "Gis.

4

Aimee," my dad's family went to a small Adventist church. They continued to attend because the pastor and some of the members were very accepting of the Pentecostal experience.

One of the reasons I am giving the spiritual background of my family is because it gives an understanding of the unusual "mix" of music, doctrine, and organization of individual churches in what we call "early Pentecost." For instance, the church I grew up in tolerated a number of people who leaned toward eternal security as long as they believed in speaking in tongues and living a "separated life." Others were Adventists and believed in the "sleep of the dead" until the coming of Christ.

My father claimed to be what was called at the time "Canadian Oneness," probably because of the influence of Aimee Semple McPherson who had a Canadian background. They believed in the Father, Son, and Holy Spirit; but they believed everything you did was to be done in Jesus' name. Some baptized using the formula, "I now baptize you in Jesus' name into the Father and the Son and the Holy Ghost." I was baptized in Jesus' name without reference to the Trinity.

Some of the strong Jesus Only people were very radical and legalistic. I knew of a number of them who had their baptismal tanks painted red because they taught a person was not saved unless they were baptized in Jesus' name. The red, of course, signified the blood of Jesus.

Others of that group taught that a person not only had to be baptized in Jesus' name but also had to receive the baptism of the Holy Spirit with the evidence of speaking in tongues in order to be saved. They based their doctrine on such biblical statements as "one Lord, one faith, one baptism."

My Grandfather Crabtree was a very strong Jesus Only believer who worried a bit about my father's tolerance of Trinitarians. My brother David loved to "press his

5

button" concerning the Oneness doctrine; and on one occasion I heard "Grampy Crabtree" yell at my brother, "You can have your three gods, and I'll take me one!" and proceeded to stomp out of the room.

In Maine, the arguments between the Trinitarians and the Jesus Only people caused constant tension in my Pentecostal world. I well remember hearing of Oneness preachers in Maine and New Brunswick, Canada, publicly denouncing my father from their pulpits as a compromiser and a preacher of heresy. Those reports hurt me tremendously because I knew my father better than any of his critics and knew he lived a life above reproach. He started every day at 5 o'clock in the morning for an hour in prayer and spent another hour later in the day reading and studying the scripture. Early in life I learned that Bible truth in the hands of a mean, insecure Pentecostal with a critical spirit does more harm to the Pentecostal church than anyone else. It is my deep conviction the Pentecostal church as a whole too often emphasized the gifts of the Spirit to the near exclusion of the fruit of the Spirit.

If I were given the opportunity to begin my Pentecostal ministry again, I would put a much greater emphasis on the enablement of the Spirit to overcome evil and build character. Jesus Himself began His earthly ministry by resisting satanic temptation. Throughout the 20th century, the Pentecostal church was unnecessarily damaged by gifted "miracle workers" who were greedy for fame and money and, in some cases, were immoral. Jesus was very clear to warn us that there would come many using His name as their authority to perform miracles such as healing the sick and casting out devils as proof of divine approval; but at the final judgment Jesus will say, "I never knew you. Away from me, you evildoers!" (Matthew 7:23 NIV).

Please pardon the interruption of the rather long explanation of the Pentecostal culture into which I was born and raised, but I felt it was important for you to gain some insight into why there was so much misunderstanding even to this day of the Pentecostal Movement. I now return to my father's spiritual journey.

Some months after the Aimee Semple McPherson tent meeting, two of my father's friends who later became missionaries to Africa invited my dad to go with them on a trip to Macon, Georgia. One of them had a connection to an early Pentecostal leader, Professor Rufus Mosley who lived in Macon. Mosley authored the book, *Manifest Destiny*, which 50 years later would become a best seller during the Charismatic Renewal. As a little boy, I remember him when he came to preach for my father; and to put it mildly, I thought he was really odd. He came with two large suitcases, one of them filled with nuts and grains. He ate very little of our food. I confess in carnal moments that the statement, "You are what you eat," applied somewhat to the good professor.

The trip to Georgia proved to be a dramatic turning point in my father's life. While there, he met a set of unmarried older twins, Carro and Susie Davis. Carro was the principal of a public grade school, and Susie was a teacher in the same school. The Davis family was quite wealthy and influential in Macon. The brother of the twins would later become a senator.

The Davis sisters had become rather influential Pentecostal leaders in Macon under Professor Mosley with no thought of leaving Georgia; but during the visit of the three young men from Maine, they believed God had spoken to Carro and confirmed by Susie they were to leave Georgia and take the Pentecostal message to Maine and northeastern Canada. They also believed my father was to minister with them as their assistant, and he felt it was God's will for him as well. My dad's two friends returned to Maine, leaving him in Macon to help the Davis sisters prepare to make the move to the northeast. My dad said

7

that it was no problem for him because all he owned fit in one cardboard suitcase.

It is difficult for me to understand the total obedience to the leading of the Lord by the Davis sisters as well as my father—a very unlikely trio consisting of two highly educated twins from Georgia and a poor, uneducated farm boy from Maine. They traveled along the east coast until they came to Maine. They did not know if they were to start a church in Maine or New Brunswick, Canada, first so they decided to travel until God told them to stop. When they came to the outskirts of Bangor, Maine, Carro told them God had just spoken to her and they were to plant a church in Bangor.

My father told me that helping to start the church in Bangor was one of the most difficult assignments he ever had. They began the church with street meetings in the middle of the winter. It was brutal; but by the spring, they had a group of people who helped them secure a building and the Bangor Pentecostal Assembly (not affiliated with the Assemblies of God) was organized. It is unclear how long they stayed in Bangor, but it was months—not years—when Carro again felt strongly that the Lord had told her it was time to move to St. John, New Brunswick, and start a new Pentecostal "work." They left the Bangor church in the hands of a young preacher from the area and proceeded to Canada.

Soon after the Davis sisters and my father arrived in St. John, a true revival started which resulted in several hundred people receiving the Pentecostal experience and becoming a part of the new church. They started in a small hall, then rented the Masons' auditorium, and soon after secured a permanent building. It would become the largest Pentecostal church in New Brunswick for many years.

Because of the success of the St. John church, the Davis sisters along with my father as their chauffeur were invited to minister throughout the province of New Brunswick to Pentecostal groups wanting to establish churches. Most of the time they met in homes. On one occasion, they were invited to minister to a group of about 20 in Bathurst. In the group was a young lady, Mary Helen Eddy, who would become my mother. She told me that the young man who would later become my father had been battling the flu and looked rather "peaked." She had not been impressed but he had certainly taken notice, and the romance began.

My mother was born in Bathurst, New Brunswick, Canada, the daughter of George Eddy, a wealthy business man whom I never met. His main business was the Eddy Lumber Company, but he also was a bit of an entrepreneur and founded the Eddy Company which operated a lumber mill, a saw mill, a carriage shop, and even a flour mill. The company still exists under the name, The Eddy Group. My mother told me he was a no-nonsense boss, both at home and in his businesses. If he caught any of his employees lounging around at the job site, he would fire them on the spot. She loved to tell me about the time he went to Detroit to visit with Henry Ford about establishing a possible distributorship in New Brunswick (which did not work out). Ford put him in a "fancy" hotel with a bathroom that had a funny looking thing sticking out of the wall. "What's that thing?" he demanded. The porter answered and said, "Well, Mr. Eddy, it is called a shower; and what you do instead of taking a bath is to stand under it, turn the nozzles, and water will come out." My grandfather said, "Sounds good." Some time later, the hotel staff was shocked to hear about a man in the hallway wearing only a towel yelling, "That thing is only good for scalding pigs!" He had turned on the hot water not knowing he needed to adjust the temperature with the cold-water tap. My mother told me he had no patience. He paid no attention to street signs or speed limits when driving. On two occasions, the car he was driving got stuck in the mud. He kept "the pedal to the metal" and proceeded to blow the engines. He had little interest in anything religious but attended the Methodist church from time to time on special occasions for the sake of his family but was, to say the least, far from a model Christian.

My Grandmother Eddy was a wonderful Christian. In spite of her husband's lack of interest in the things of God, she insisted all eleven of her children attend the church faithfully. Because of her faith, several of her children were devout Christians all their lives.

In later years, she lived with one of her daughters (Aunt Avie Sprague) in St. John, New Brunswick, Canada, about 200 miles from Bangor where Dad pastored soon after I was born. Early one morning on Labor Day we received word to come quickly because she was dying. It took less than an hour for our family to get on the road in our trusty 1941 Plymouth sedan. We had hardly gotten started when Dad announced that we were going to go to St. John by way of the Airline Road. I will never forget the collective "oh" from my brother and sister riding in the back seat. The Airline Road cut off about two hours of travel time, but very little of it was paved and there was only one gas station halfway to the Canadian border (about 90 miles).

The trip to St. John went quite well. We took note the gas station was closed, and Dad remarked it was unusual for it not to be open on a holiday. About five miles past the gas station, we hit a pretty bad rut in the dirt road and our car sagged to a stop. My dad jumped out and, after looking under the car, announced that the spring had broken. I will never forget my mom's bursting into tears (it was like it happened yesterday) and saying, "I'll never see Mother alive again." My dad reached over, put his arm around her, and said, "Now Helen, the Lord knows all about it." Turning to us, he said, "Okay, children, let's get out and pray."

It must have been quite an interesting sight to see two adults and three kids standing by the side of the road with bowed heads holding hands in prayer. I do not remember much of Dad's prayer, but I do remember that in just a few minutes he stopped rather abruptly and said, "I believe the Lord heard us, and we'll be fine." It was not too long after we heard someone coming up behind us traveling pretty fast. It looked like he was going to go right past us in the pickup truck he was driving but came to a stop several yards beyond our "sick" car. It turned out the driver was the owner of the gas station. We knew in a very short time he was not an angel because of the language he used to express his outrage at his wife who had taken his car to Bangor with all of his fishing equipment in the trunk. After venting his anger a few seconds, he said, "Okay, what have we got here?" After looking at our disabled car, he shook his head and said, "I don't think I can help you. You've got a broken spring and I'm not sure I've got one back at the station that will fit, but let me see what I've got in the back of the pickup." When he came back from looking, my dad would later say that he was a man in shock. I do remember his saying, "Someone is sure looking out for you people. All I've got in the pickup is my tool box, a jack, and a spring that looks like it will fit." It did not seem very long before we were on our way. To add to the miracle, the garage owner refused to take a penny for the spring or his labor. Mother made it to St. John in time to spend several hours at my grandmother's bedside before she died.

When my mother finished high school in Bathurst, she was sent to Montreal, Quebec, to what was called a "finishing school." Those schools prepared young ladies from well-to-do homes to become professionals in "proper" careers such as teachers or executive secretaries.

According to my mother, she planned to return to Bathurst and become part of the family business.

One summer Sunday night in Montreal, my mother and two of her friends were walking down the street and heard singing coming from the open windows of a church. The girls decided to go in and listen for a few minutes. After the song service was over, two of the girls wanted to leave, but my mother wanted to stay. She told the girls to go on and she would catch up to them at the school dorm located just a few blocks from the church, and that is what they did.

My mother stayed to listen to the pastor preach. At the end of the sermon, he gave an altar appeal; and my mother said she was so convicted of her sin she responded quickly. She told me that after praying for some time, she felt a peace she had never known. She knew without a doubt she was a true born-again Christian. She does not remember how long she was at the altar but became aware that most of the congregation had left. As she prepared to get up from the altar, the pastor, known in our family as "Daddy Baker," came to her for the purpose of helping her understand what she had just experienced and give her counsel on how to deepen her walk with God. After talking with her for some time, he told her she was in a Pentecostal church which believed every born-again Christian should receive the baptism of the Holy Spirit with the initial physical evidence of speaking with a heavenly language. When Mother was asked if she desired to receive the baptism, she told Daddy Baker she "wanted everything God had" for her. He then proceeded to lay hands on her head and pray. It was her testimony that the first person she ever heard speak in tongues was herself.

My mother finished her course at the finishing school and returned to Bathurst to work in the office at the Eddy Lumber Company. Her testimony of salvation and the

Pentecostal experience was no problem with her mother and a couple of her sisters; but her father, in her words, was beyond furious. For all intents and purposes, he disowned her, especially after she married my father—the rather sick-looking young man she first met at the house meeting in Bathurst. The marriage got off to a rather unusual start. On the one-day honeymoon, Mother was driving her car (Dad did not own one) too fast like her father, did not slow down to take a curve in the road, and succeeded in flipping the car. Miraculously, neither the car nor the passengers were seriously damaged or hurt; but Mother never applied for a new driver's license or drove again for the rest of her life.

Dad was still the assistant pastor to the Davis sisters at a salary of $1 a week. His only dress-up suit was a combination of "hand-me-downs" from some of the men in the church consisting of black pants, a dark brown coat, and a dark green vest so he had the whole lot dyed black. The Davis sisters raised the salary to $5 a week for the young couple; but of course, it was not enough even in those days for them to rent their own place so they had to move in with the sisters. My mother knew the old maid sisters resented her, and Carro especially was not very kind. After several months, the situation got so bad that my father decided to have pity on my mother and accepted an invitation to start a new church in a place called Hatfield Point, New Brunswick. It was very hard at first. My dad and mom had a miserable place to live. (They were so poor that they covered the windows with newspapers in place of curtains). In spite of the poverty, my mother told me it "was like heaven after living with the Davis sisters."

A few months after starting the church in Hatfield Point, a true revival broke out and people from all over the county began to be saved. It was said that the time came when you could not drive over a mile in any direction without passing a house occupied by a family that attended the new church.

My father told me that for seven months the Lord would not let him preach about the baptism in the Holy Spirit. Every day he would pray that God would let him preach the next Sunday about Pentecost, but every day the only word he heard in his spirit was "wait." Word began to spread that my father was no longer a Pentecostal but a compromiser. One Sunday night, God decided to vindicate my father's patience and obedience. At the altar service, three men were praying together when suddenly the power of God struck all of them at once and they began speaking in other tongues. My dad told me that God said to him, "You can now preach the Pentecostal message." He did, and the church became thoroughly Pentecostal. A few months later my mother became pregnant with her first child.

In St. John, the Davis sisters were finding it very difficult to pastor without my father as their assistant. They were also a bit upset (maybe jealous?) about the great revival in Hatfield Point.

One day they drove to Hatfield Point to talk to my folks. My mother said she had never seen Carro so humble. She told my dad that she and Susie had not treated them right; and if they would come back to St. John, they would provide them with their own house and a decent salary. They also brought up the fact that my mother needed to be in St. John near good medical facilities to have the baby. In spite of my mother's reluctance, my dad felt a strong loyalty and obligation to the Davis sisters and proceeded to resign the church and move back to St. John.

For approximately three years, my parents served as assistant pastors to the Davis sisters after they resigned from Hatfield Point. During those three years, my mother gave birth to my brother, David Clifford, and my sister, Hazel Elizabeth. From what I understand, my father did his best to serve the church in St. John; but the experience in Hatfield Point had given him a desire to pastor again. Furthermore, he knew my mother was not happy so when they received an invitation to pastor the Pentecostal church on Grand Manon Island, Nova Scotia, they accepted the call.

My father always said they were out of God's will moving to Grand Manon. He felt the reason he accepted the pastorate there was simply to get out of St. John. The church was very small, and they struggled just to have enough food to eat. Dad would walk down to the docks nearly every evening when the boats came in, and invariably one of the fisherman would toss him a fresh haddock free of charge. I cannot imagine anyone getting sick of eating fresh haddock right out of the cold waters of the Atlantic, but my folks did. I guess too much of anything is too much.

While in Grand Manon, my mother gave birth to her third child, Esther Mae. They often spoke of what a beautiful baby she was and how much joy she brought to them while living in such a difficult situation. When the baby was nine months old, my folks visited Halifax, Nova Scotia, to attend a church convention. They left the children in the care of one of the young ladies from the church who stayed at the parsonage. When my parents returned from the convention, they discovered that Esther was very sick with pneumonia. They took her to St. John to the hospital, but she died a few hours after she was admitted. One can hardly imagine the sorrow of my parents. To add to the tragedy, they did not even have enough money to buy her a grave marker.

Soon after Esther Mae died, my folks were called to pastor the Pentecostal church in Provincetown, Prince Edward Island. They had a good ministry there; but after serving for only about a year, they felt very strongly to take the Full Gospel Church in Halifax, Nova Scotia—under very unusual circumstances. It had been a rather prominent Baptist church for many years, but a Pentecostal evangelist came to the city and was used of God with miraculous results. Scores of people were dramatically healed and even a greater number were filled with the Holy Spirit with the evidence of speaking in other tongues, among them a significant number from the Baptist church both in the leadership and the membership. The church split with more than half the congregation wanting it to be Pentecostal. The pastor had received the baptism, but he did not feel he was the one to lead the church and called my father whom he had heard was a very effective Pentecostal leader. My father had a wonderful ministry in Halifax. Through the Lord's help, he was able to bring healing to the congregation and changed the name to Full Gospel Assembly (not affiliated with the Assemblies of God). The church itself became known as one of the first "Bapticostal" churches in history, and my mother became a true co-pastor with my father and built a very strong Sunday School.

Soon after arriving in Halifax, a babysitter decided to take David for a walk in his stroller in a park near the house. Two large dogs were turned loose, and they came running and barking at the sitter. It scared her so badly she turned loose of the stroller which proceeded to take off down the hill and turn over, spilling my brother out on the ground. Before people could get the dogs off, they had playfully mauled David and pushed him down the hill. He was not hurt physically; but from that day on, he had an abnormal fear of dogs to the point where my parents held him back from starting school for a year so Hazel could walk with him. We had a great time teasing him every once in a while to remind him he still needed his little sister to be his guardian.

It was in the parsonage in Halifax, Nova Scotia, I was born.

# CHAPTER 2

When I was two and a half years old, my father received a rather desperate call for him to leave Halifax and come back to Bangor, Maine, and assume the pastorate of the church he and the Davis sisters had started on the street corner before going to St. John. To say there was a church there was a bit of a stretch. After the Davis sisters and Dad left, the church had met with some success; but because of some doctrinal issues, the church eventually split three ways and only a handful remained of the original group. My mother told me that my dad loved to run away from every success and tackle the worst possible situation, but Bangor would prove to be the exception. They would stay for over 30 years and live out the rest of their pastoral lives.

During the time I was growing up, Bangor was a city of approximately 30,000 people with a town of about half that size directly across on the banks of the Penobscot River called Brewer. They were called twin cities by some, and I used to like to say that Bangor was the "fat lady" and Brewer was the "skinny lady" who smelled bad because of the big pulp mill situated on the river across from Bangor. During the summer, the river was always chocked full of logs ready to be processed into paper. In his book, *The Hunt for Red October*, Tom Clancy decided to end his epic fictional tale about a Russian sub that ended up downriver from Bangor/Brewer in the waters of the Penobscot.

The fact that I was the youngest brother of two very aggressive and talented siblings added to the natural feeling of inferiority from the beginning. My brother David was at once a delight and a threat to a little brother. He learned to be an outstanding trombonist at a very early age and was part of our church "orchestra" and a trombone soloist for as long as I could remember. Like myself, he had no interest in school but found a way to make life interesting. He had a knack of teasing me to death. One of my earliest memories was the time David, almost nine years old, was helping my dad repair a broken door in the house by handing him tools. I was four. Of course, I was watching the whole thing with interest; but David kept bugging me with questions like "wanna fight" or "wanna wrestle" until I had had enough and yelled, "I'll wrestle ya," and launched into the air, sending him and his stupid tools flying. To put it mildly, he was in total shock; and my dad could hardly get back to work for laughing. I felt great for several days and still do when I think about it.

My sister Hazel became a fine pianist at a rather early age. She was a very good student and was a bit kinder to me than David (which did not take much effort). She and David became a very well-known duet and were asked to perform often at our church and even other churches in the area. It is important for me to say at this point that I idolized my brother. I used to say that I loved my brother because he teased the devil out of me.

One of my first memories was receiving a toy medical doctor's kit Christmas morning 1940. I pestered everybody in the house to let me "examine" them. For many years after, I dreamed of becoming a doctor.

At the age of four, I was enrolled in kindergarten which was a mistake for two reasons: I was small for my age, and I had not had much contact with anyone my age outside the church. I learned very quickly that kids can be very cruel to those who are not part of their world. In my case, I did not know anyone in my class; and for some reason, they thought our Pentecostal church was some kind of a weird Jewish sect. One day at recess near the first of the school year, they surrounded me and began to chant, "Jew, Jew; you're a Jew. We're gonna spit all over you!" After a few chants, a teacher came running over and gave them a tongue lashing. They never did it again; and to this day, I have a soft spot in my heart for that teacher.

The early years of growing up in the Pentecostal movement did have what some would call a negative effect upon me psychologically. Besides being the youngest and the smallest kid in the class, I was not allowed to participate in any sports outside my gym classes or attend any "worldly" events such as ballgames so you can imagine how proud I was in the third grade to become a "patrol boy." My job was to stand at one of the crosswalks near the school and make sure it was safe for kids to cross the street. I wore a wide white belt around my waist and over my shoulder with a big silver badge. You can be sure I polished that badge to the highest shine.

I tended to find ways to minimize criticism and avoid conflict of any kind. I learned that an acceptable escape was reading but not with anything to do with school work. There was absolutely no reason to learn any of the subjects because there was no incentive. I was not shown what good any of it would do for someone who could not be involved in sports or prepare to live a "godless life" or prepare to be a success in a "worldly profession," so I took all kinds of fiction to read on the sly in class. I read every one of the Hardy Boys books, even some of my sister's Nancy Drew mysteries, and every conceivable detective series. I had a very active library card and became an advanced reader for my age. I did get in some trouble at times with teachers who caught me reading a mystery while they were trying to teach. Occasionally, they gave me detention which I would use as an opportunity to finish a mystery.

My reading obsession continued at home. My parents believed kids should get to bed early and get up early. I still do not agree with them because some kids are "wired" differently from others. I hated to go to bed but also hated to get up early. I learned to hide a flashlight under my blankets so I could later cover my head and read a smuggled book until I got tired enough to go to sleep. (I thought it was pretty clever because I could turn the light off without getting out of bed.) I read most of *The Count of Monte Cristo* and several others using that method.

My other escape was music. In no way was it as much fun as my reading adventures, but learning to play sacred and classical music was an acceptable outlet for a Pentecostal preacher's son. I became an usher for the Bangor Symphony Orchestra when they performed on evenings we did not have church. I still have a deep appreciation for classical music.

For some reason I became interested in playing the marimba so my parents sent me to the Bangor Conservatory of Music once a week to take lessons from a very fine marimbist. He was the first pipe smoker I knew, and I can still smell the wonderful odors of some of the exotic tobacco he enjoyed. I learned more about tobacco from him than how to play the marimba (my folks would have gone ballistic if they had known). If I had not learned that "all smokers go to hell," I would be a pipe-smoking aficionado to this day.

I still laugh thinking about the time my dad was in downtown Bangor and saw a well-known hypocrite who visited our church from time to time smoking a cigarette some distance away. Dad made a point to "accidentally" run into him. When the guy saw Dad coming, he hurriedly stuffed the cigarette into his pants pocket hoping to move on quickly, but Dad kept him in conversation for quite a while. Dad reported he had never seen anyone so uncomfortable and was sure the poor victim burned a bit of a hole in his pants.

You will have to pardon my mentioning some of the unpleasant sides of my early years as a Pentecostal pastor's son, but I want you to understand that there is a negative side of Pentecostal history. In my opinion, however, it is far outweighed by the overall incredible work of the Holy Spirit in so much of our early twentieth century history as well as in my own personal story. In other words, I know many people were turned off by the negative and God will have to judge all of that, but I saw so much that was truly supernatural and positive that I can overlook a lot of human foibles, including my own.

It is a bit amusing for me to look back on my childhood and remember some of the bad things I did. I learned very early in life to do my sinning very secretly because I watched my brother get punished over and over because he did not use any wisdom in pursuing his "career of crime." One time when I was four, a little neighbor girl who knew I was a preacher's son said, "Bet you don't know how to swear." I said, "Yes, I do." "No, you don't!" "Do too!" She then said, "Prove it!" I looked all around, opened the back door of our car, and told her to get in. I shut the door and whispered, "Damn." Her eyes got really big, and she proceeded to take off. I got ready to go to the lake of fire that burns forever and ever.

One time while visiting my cousin Wayne on his family farm in Aroostook County, we got the brilliant idea to try smoking. There were no cigarettes available so we used our genius to make our own by wrapping some hay chaff in some brown paper and lighting up behind the barn. We both got pretty nauseated and came close to throwing up. I have never ever had a desire to smoke since.

When I was a little past my fifth birthday, I was genuinely saved following a Sunday afternoon service. I remember that during my father's sermon, I was gripped by an almost overwhelming sense of conviction for my "long life of sin and crime." During the closing prayer, I snuck out of the front seat and made my way to the balcony area. I did that because I was certain no one would take me seriously and I did not want to be misunderstood. I went into a very appropriate place to get saved and cleaned up—a large janitor's closet. I can remember the entire incident as if it were yesterday. I cried and asked Jesus to please forgive me of all my sins. I repeated the prayer several times until I suddenly felt a wonderful peace. There was no audible voice; but I knew beyond a shadow of a doubt that Jesus loved me and if I died, I would go to heaven. Because of my shyness, I did not tell anyone. Near the house, I could not keep it in any longer and blurted out words such as, "I asked Jesus to forgive me and He did." I was shocked by the response of my parents. They both believed me and told me how happy they were. I do not remember if Hazel or David said anything because I was so happy Dad and Mom believed me. That experience was so real and dramatic to me personally that it has been an anchor for my faith all my life.

At the next announcement of a water baptism, I told my folks I wanted to be baptized. My dad told me he would think about it. Later I found out that he and my mom had a little argument over it. My dad wanted to have me wait until I was older, but my mom thought it would be the worst possible decision. It was one of the many times my mom would go to bat for me and, as usual, she won. Our water baptisms were held twice a year on the banks of the Kenduskeag River. The first baptism of the year was the Sunday after Easter. It was a full-blown service with songs and scripture reading. My dad would then walk out into the stream which was about waist high, and the candidates got in line along the bank and he would call for them one by one. I hate to admit it, but the only thing I remember about my baptism was thinking that I had never been so cold in my life. At least I was ready to die. At the same baptism, the whole crowd was shocked when one of the new Christians who did not know better took the bath towel given to each candidate when they came out of the water and proceeded to take his pants off the minute he got out of the water and dry himself off in front of everyone instead of moving behind a tree. He did keep his boxer shorts on which really helped.

It reminds me of the baptism one of my acquaintances held on the banks of the Jordan River in Israel which is a tradition for most Christian tour groups. One of the women forgot to secure her wig tightly enough, and it came off when she was baptized and began floating down the river. That was funny enough, but her husband jumped into the river and retrieved it after a short swim. I guess he did not want to buy her another one.

A lot of funny things have happened at water baptisms. Hugh Rosenberg, one of my pastor friends, told me he was about to baptize a young lady with special needs. He noticed when he began to recite the words, "Upon the confession of your faith, etc.," she would immediately start holding her breath. Knowing she would not be able to hold it long enough to get through the whole process, he would start over after telling her to wait to hold her breath until she was ready to be immersed. After three or four attempts, she finally said in a rather loud voice before taking a deep breath, "Let 'er rip!" I guess she survived.

One of our friends was asked to take a photograph of a family member when she was baptized. He stood too close to the top of the stairs going into the baptismal tank and proceeded to fall in, camera and all. He made quite a splash. Reminds me of what happened to the famous preacher, Robert G. Lee, when he stood too close to the grave opening at a committal service and fell into the grave and slipped under the casket. If that had happened to me, I might have told them to just go ahead and bury me with the deceased.

From time to time when I was quite young, a very famous woman preacher at the time, Christine Gibson, visited our home. She was the president of Zion Bible Institute in East Providence, Rhode Island. Zion was a true "faith school" that charged no tuition and paid the faculty no salaries. Every year during potato harvest in Aroostook County, Maine, the farmers would fill a box car or trailer full of potatoes and send it to the school where the potatoes were stored in the basements of the seven or eight houses serving as dorms. It became known as the "starchiest" school in the world because at times potatoes were all the food the students had to eat. Sis. Gibson, as she was called, would stop by our home on her trip to Aroostook to thank the farmers because our home was almost exactly half way to her destination. On two of those occasions, I remember her coming to the door accompanied by two or three of her staff, causing quite a stir. I recall standing back in the hall watching with great shyness all the important people hugging and carrying on; but then Sis. Gibson, on those two occasions, saw me over the shoulder of my mother and proceeded to move around her and came to where I was and literally knelt down in front of me, pressed a little bag of pennies in my hand, and said, "Here's my preacher boy. Now, Charles, you get ready to be a man of God." On many occasions while shaving, I would set aside the razor and say, "Now, Charles, you get ready to be a man of God today."

One of the blessings (and sometimes not) of growing up in a Pentecostal pastor's home was the fact that there was never a thought of putting up guest preachers in a hotel (unnecessary waste of God's money) or in a member's home (too risky) so all visiting preachers wound up staying at our house sometimes for two or three weeks. We had "protracted" revival meetings a minimum of two times a year plus the fall convention.

You cannot imagine the varied and unique personalities that came to live with us every year. It would probably not shock you to know that I hardly remember how good any of them preached; but after less than a week of living with us, I had a pretty accurate idea of how good a person they were, and that was about a thousand times more important to a young boy than how brilliant they were in the pulpit. I am convinced that I am a Christian today because of my early home life and not my church life. Furthermore, I believe I am a Christian today because I lived with godly, consistent parents who were more influential than any famous preachers who lived with us a few days or preached from my dad's pulpit.

I relate wholeheartedly to the story of the young man who was raised in a Christian home but decided to forsake the church and live a godless life. Soon after his father's death, he came back to God and the church. One of the church members asked him this question, "Was it your father's death that brought you back to faith in Christ?" to which he answered, "No, it was his life."

It will probably amuse you to know that when I was a small boy growing up in a parsonage, I did not know my dad's profession. When I first went to public school, the teacher asked us what our parents did for a living. As the kids began to answer, I was in a panic because I had no idea what my folks did for a living because they were either at home or at church. I suddenly remembered my dad went to a radio station every week to record a program of some kind so I proudly announced my dad was a radio announcer.

One of the most dramatic periods in my life happened when I was about six years old. My mother had a complete nervous breakdown that put her in bed for two or three months. (It seemed to me like two or three years).

Looking back, I understand quite clearly why she collapsed. She carried all the duties of a mother plus the hard work of a hotelier for several weeks a year, having the responsibility to provide a clean bedroom and three meals a day for guests as well as being a co-pastor with my dad with no pay. Her role in the church was running the Sunday School and teaching the Adult Bible Class.

Then came word that one of her favorite sisters, Hazel, was very sick with a fast-moving cancer. She and my mother had a special bond (my own sister had been named in her honor). In a few weeks Aunt Hazel died. When Mother returned from the funeral in Canada, she was not the same. In a matter of days, she became bedfast in serious depression.

You cannot imagine the change in the Crabtree household when Mother took sick. Later I was to find out that the most deeply affected was my dad who had to take over all of the responsibilities of Mother both at church and in the home. In those early days there was little help from the congregation. I will never forget the figure of my dad kneeling at Mother's bedside asking God to heal her. The Lord answered my father's prayers in a rather unique way.

One day as I was playing with some toy cars near Mother's bed, she said to me, "Charles, bring me that piece of paper stuck on the stove." It was a little Franklin wood-burning stove used during the winter months to heat the bedroom. I looked and saw a round piece of black paper stuck between the grate and the body of the stove. When I gave it to her, she began to cry and praise the Lord. Of course, I did not understand at the time, but I later learned it was from the weekly scripture verse printed in the *Pentecostal Evangel.* Someone had cut it out and left it in the bedroom. We never knew who did it. The scripture portion read, "I am the          that healeth thee" (Exodus 15:26 KJV).

It was only a couple of days after we first saw the scripture portion that Mother was able to go to the back-yard and sit for a period of time on a wooden lawn chair. While sitting there, a gust of wind blew a round piece of black paper from near the fence and it came to rest next to her chair. Of course, it was the same piece of paper. We have no idea how in the world it got there.

She was immediately strengthened. The next day she was able to go for a ride in our 1941 Plymouth sedan. As she prepared to get in the front seat, she burst into praise, speaking in tongues because between the running board and the body of the car was the same piece of paper: "I am the Lord that healeth thee," and indeed, He did. My mother enjoyed wonderful health overall for many years.

The years from kindergarten to junior high hold very few memorable events for me outside the home and the church. The routine in the home was very seldom inter-rupted except for ministerial guests. During the school year, I would be awakened early, especially when my sib-lings went to high school. Their school day started with first classes set for exactly 7:35. They would be given 20 minutes for lunch and dismissed at 1:30 so kids could hold down a part-time job. Because we Crabtree kids had to get dressed, have breakfast and devotions, and then walk a little over a mile, we had to rise and shine no later than 6. My grade school day started at 9 and ended at 3:30; but because Hazel and David had to be at their school early, I became the victim of their schedule for sev-eral years. My dad was not about to prepare breakfast and have devotions just for me so I had to join Hazel and David for breakfast and family devotions. My mother did not like to eat before 8 so Dad was assigned the wonderful task to take care of us during school days. His breakfasts were normally pretty awful. I'm sure my memory settles on early morning negativity, but I do remember we had to have either Cream of Wheat or Cream of Rice several times a week because they were cheap and he liked them. The only problem was that he invariably cooked them too fast and did not stir them much in the cooking so they always had lumps. It took me many years after leaving home to even have breakfast, and it was almost 30 years before I found out Cream of Wheat and Cream of Rice tasted good if they were cooked properly.

When school was not in session, the schedule at home was a lot better. We were allowed to sleep in until 7 o'clock, and Mother cooked breakfast. What a difference a cook makes. When we did not have school, breakfast was at 8 o'clock sharp followed by everyone meeting for family devotions which could run 30 minutes plus. For 99 percent plus of the population, my life growing up would have been pure torture; but with the love of my family and some folks in the church, I found life to be quite pleasant.

During the winter months which were sometimes brutal, we would build great snow forts and have snowball fights, build giant snowmen, and go ice skating on the river behind our house when there was not too much snow. Otherwise, my brother and I would clear a large area of the frozen lawn in the backyard and build banks of snow all around the leveled area. We would wait for the temperature to rise to the mid-thirties in the middle of an afternoon and take a hose to create a small but beautiful rink that we could use up to a month at a time in really cold weather. We often had lots of snow in Bangor. I can remember times when people would tie little red flags on top of their radio antennas so people could see them around street corners.

To tell the truth, I was so cut off from the "real world" I had no idea what I was missing. My mother was really a life saver. She insisted her children play lots of table games and put big puzzles together, and she also provided a week of vacation. She would say to my dad almost every year, "We need to take the family away for a week this summer and let the children swim and fish." Of course, we would never stay over a Sunday. I remember one time she said that to him, and he looked at her very puzzled. He said so sincerely, "I do not understand why you think it is necessary to pack up this family and go halfway around the world (the farthest we ever went was less than 100 miles from home) when we have perfectly good beds at home. Furthermore, it is a waste of God's money to pay for a cabin." Mother knew how to handle Dad. She would say, "Well, Clifford, let's pray someone will offer us a cabin for nothing; and if that would happen, let's accept that as the will of God this year." He would say something like, "If that would happen, I would accept that as the will of God." Mother would not only pray but would also go right to work without dad's knowing it to make it happen. A month or two later she would come to Dad in the presence of the kids to say, "Praise the Lord, Clifford, so-and-so has offered to loan us their cabin this summer." We kids would all cheer, and even he could not deny the joy and exuberance it brought to the family. Mother was smart.

One place we really enjoyed from time to time was Blue Hill, Maine, which had a beautiful lake. One Friday afternoon at the end of our vacation, David and I were fishing for sun perch on top of a huge rock within wading distance from the shore when Hazel came down from the cabin to spy on us to hopefully be able to report to the folks about some terrible misdeed we had committed. Near the shore was a rocky bank. She tripped and fell hard. We heard her screaming, dropped our poles, and scrambled off the rock as fast as we could. We were really scared because we saw a lot of blood on the side of the leg she had skinned while falling. We got on either side of her and, as best we could, carried and dragged her back to the cabin. We took the most direct route which we had no way of knowing was full of poison ivy. My mother did her best to clean up the wound, but it was not long until it was apparent Hazel had a serious infection. It became a real crisis when the doctor informed my folks that it looked like drastic action might be needed to save Hazel's life. If the infection moved further up her leg, he would have to amputate it a little below the hip. Dad asked, "How long do you think we have?" The doctor said, "I will probably have to make a decision as early as tomorrow." My mother said the doctor looked at my father really funny when he said, "Good, that will give us time to take Hazel's situation to the Great Physician."

When Mom and Dad came home and informed us what the doctor had said, my dad told us that Mother and he were going right to prayer and we should go ahead and get ourselves some cereal if we got hungry. Mom and Dad's prayer room consisted of two overstuffed chairs in their bedroom upstairs. David and I did get some cereal and then went to the living room to cut out the pictures of the new cars coming out in the fall. All that time we heard Mom and Dad calling on God upstairs. One hour, then two, and into the third hour we heard it! Shouts of victory! The folks had just "prayed through." I remember my brother winked at me. We knew what was coming. Maybe two minutes after the shout, Dad came downstairs and said, "All right boys, it's time for you to go to bed. Mother and I have prayed through, and Hazel will be fine." Of course, she was! When the doctor examined Hazel the next morning, my folks said he could not believe what had happened. He had never seen infection that serious clear up so fast. My dad said he reminded the doctor he was going to take Hazel's case to another physician.

There were times I was amazed at my father's faith, but I believe the secret of his faith was his love for souls. He witnessed everywhere. My brother and I would get frustrated when he would always take time to witness to the gas station attendant when he went to fill up the car.

One time my smart-aleck brother said, "Dad, could we just have the car filled up without having an evangelistic crusade?" There were several times I remember seeing him prostrate on the carpet at prayer meeting saying, "God, give me souls. I would rather die than to go on in ministry without seeing souls saved." The Lord did answer his prayer many times. I witnessed many dramatic conversions.

It has been a temptation through the years for me to look back and point out what was wrong with "old-time Pentecostals." In my opinion, they were too legalistic and fearful of "too much education" and personal counseling; but overall, they were far ahead of me in love for God, bible study, prayer, and character.

In these days, my father would not be considered a "real" student. He had a few books apart from the Bible: a *Cruden's Concordance* and *Fox's Book of Martyrs*. He also enjoyed a magazine called "The Golden Grain," a monthly publication put out by Charles Price, and a few books by Vance Havner and Clovis Chapell. That was about it. I laughed when my brother David told me that when he first showed Dad his own extensive library, Dad looked over his glasses, pointed at the library, and said, "Let me tell you, I know some things that aren't in those books." And he did.

There were times I was amazed at my father's grasp of the scriptures. He knew the Word backwards and forwards, but he did have a real problem with the book of *Revelation*. He told me he got a bit of a headache trying to figure out all the beasts and dragons. When asked whether he was pre, mid, or postmillenial, he would say

"I'm pan millennial. Everything is going to 'pan' out." But overall, he not only knew the Word but also how to apply it.

The Bangor Theological Seminary was about a mile from our church. It was very liberal to the point of almost total rejection of scripture and the divinity of Christ. Students from the seminary would come to our church from time to time and corner Dad after church to ask him questions and to debate. After a period of time, the seminary absolutely forbade their students to come to Bangor Pentecostal because my dad would "confuse the students" with his biblical answers and pastoral experiences which the professors had a hard time refuting. Of course, some of them came back to visit on the sly.

My mother also had unusual wisdom in dealing with "superspiritual" people who had all kinds of strange interpretations of scripture and even dreams and visions. One time one of these people came to Mother and reported that the spirit of God had told him to take his handkerchief and tear it in four sections. He felt strongly that the Lord was telling him that the church was about to split in four ways. Mother replied that, "No, the church is not going to split in four, but the Lord might be telling you to split up the relationships between your two daughters and their unsaved boyfriends." His response was immediate: "That's it! That's it! It's a confirmation of what I have been feeling." I have no idea what came of it, but I sure admired my mother's quick answer.

My mother also had very practical wisdom in dealing with all kinds of people. There were some who came into the church from time to time who were not only unclean in their souls but also quite obviously unclean physically. Mother would prepare a paper sack filled with soap, toothbrush, toothpaste, and other good hygiene necessities and then tell them very diplomatically that the next time they came to church to be at their best, not only to worship God but also to worship with God's people. They usually did.

One time a lady known for keeping a very dirty house proudly brought "her special pie for the Crabtree family to enjoy." Mother thanked her profusely; and when she got home, she promptly put the pie in the garbage. When the lady asked Mother how the family liked her pie, Mother said, "Sister, that pie went quicker than any I can remember."

One of the greatest miracles I have ever witnessed took place in our living room when I was approximately 11 years old. The beginning of the miracle began when Dad and Mom went to see an inmate at what was then called the Bangor Insane Asylum. (they were not politically correct in those days). On the way to pray with the man they were visiting, they noticed a very beautiful young lady sitting in a wheelchair in the main hallway and remarked how sad to see anyone so young in such a tragic condition.

When my folks had ended their visit with the patient they had come to pray for, my mother said to my dad words to the effect that the Lord had told her to arrange to take the young lady to our home and minister to her. Of course, my dad was flabbergasted and reminded my mother they had no idea who the young lady was and, furthermore, they had no way to take care of her needs. My mother very seldom ever said the Lord had told her anything; but on this occasion, she assured my dad she was absolutely certain. He told her he would honor her strong assurance that God had spoken; but since it was God who had spoken to her and not to him, she would need to do the talking.

My folks decided that the first stop would have to be to the administrator of the hospital to find out the identity of the young lady. My dad told us that when they described the young woman to the administrator, he immediately knew who she was. He told them that her name was Daphine Corey from northern Maine. She had been a very brilliant student and the runner-up in the Miss Maine beauty pageant. A month or two before, she had been stricken with a very rare disease that had left her almost totally paralyzed. She was actually a patient at a Boston clinic but for a time was being treated with experimental drugs in Bangor for a few weeks to make it easier for her parents to visit her from Aroostook County, Maine.

When my mother told the administrator they were the pastors of the Bangor Pentecostal Assembly, he said quite clearly that he had heard about "you people." Mother then told him that though he might not understand, she felt strongly impressed she should take Daphine to our home to care for her. I always wished I could have been there myself to see his reaction and hear his emphatic statement that her request was absolutely impossible and he would not allow it. My mother told us that for some reason she asked the administrator how old Daphine was. He told her 17. My mother then asked the question, "Since Daphine is a minor, couldn't her parents approve her release to us if we promise to provide a nurse to follow the drug regimen?" The administrator told her that technically she was correct but he would never recommend it to her parents. On the way out of the hospital, my folks got Daphine's home address from the lady at the front desk.

When Mother got home from the hospital, she called Daphine's home and her mother answered the phone. When my mother identified who she was, Daphine's mother said, "Why, praise the Lord, Sis. Crabtree." Of course, my mother was quite shocked and asked if they had met. Mrs. Corey said, "No, but we are Pentecostal people and have visited your church a number of times when we were in the Bangor area." When Mother told her what the Lord had told her to do, there was an immediate and enthusiastic "yes" to Mother's request.

To make a long story short, Daphine was brought to our home and carried upstairs to her room. She was almost totally immobile. She had to be spoon-fed. She could not even completely change positions in her bed. A nurse came twice a day to administer her medication and make certain she was well-taken-care-of and following the pre-scribed drug regimen. Two or three times a day she was moved to a chair but that was the extent of her "activity." On the third morning of her visit, we decided to have family devotions in the living room across from Daphine's bedroom. Dad and my brother moved her to the living room and seated her on the floor with her back against the couch to change her position for a while. Dad had an emergency hospital call he needed to make and told us to go ahead with devotions and he would be back in less than an hour to help take Daphine back to her room.

When Dad left, Mother started devotions by reading a scripture and then we knelt for prayer. As usual, we kids prayed first and then Mother began to pray. Suddenly she began to pray in tongues, crawled over to Daphine, and laid her hand on her. When she did, the power of God struck.

Daphine and Mom began to praise the Lord. We watched as Daphine got to her knees and then stood to her feet and began to dance. Daphine was completely healed and later married and was the pianist for a Pen-tecostal church in Aroostook County for over 50 years. I am often amused by the reaction of people who do not believe God still performs miracles when I tell the story. They do not believe I saw what I saw. They try to explain that Daphine probably had a psychosomatic disease and for some strange reason when Mother laid her hand on her and began to praise God, Daphine responded through the power of autosuggestion. Be that as it may, I borrow the words of St. John in the introduction of his letter, "We proclaim to you what we have seen and heard" (1 John 1:3 NIV).

One of my favorite people in all the world growing up was my Grandfather Crabtree. We called him "Grampy," and he was a character. He was a widower and lived alone in a tiny, rundown farm house outside of Houlton, Maine, in Aroostook County. My cousin and I would visit him from time to time, but we did not like to spend the night because he was not much of a housekeeper, to say the least. One time we did spend the night, and the next morning Grampy decided to make us pancakes. He said, "Now boys, let me give you a little secret about making pancakes. Your mothers make a big mistake when they wash the skillet every time they use it. You will notice I haven't washed this skillet for a long time, and the pancake coating on the bottom and the edges are what help me make the best flavored pancakes in the world." To be honest, his pancakes did taste pretty good.

Grampy had a great sense of humor. He liked to tell about the time he confronted a neighbor who seemed to be depressed all the time. One day he asked the neighbor how he was doing; and the neighbor said, "Well, Dave, let me tell you, you won't be seeing me around much any longer." My grandfather asked, "Where are you going?" The neighbor said, "Never you mind." My grandfather said, "Now Al, you're not thinking of committing suicide, are you?" The neighbor just looked at him. Grampy knew the neighbor was just feeling sorry for himself and wanted attention, but Grampy would not have any of it. He said, "Now Al, if you're all set to kill yourself, let me help you. I've got a couple of sticks of dynamite. We'll put a long fuse on them, then you stick them in your pocket and run for the woods as fast as you can; and when you get there, I'll light the fuse and poof, you'll be gone. No muss, no fuss." My grandfather told me the neighbor never spoke to him again.

My family got a great kick out of the time my aunt forgot to lock the door when she went to the bathroom and Grampy walked in on her. She was shocked and so was he. She told us she had never seen anyone back out of a room as fast as he did saying, "No harm done, no harm done!" He did tell us about another neighbor who accidentally killed himself by deciding to take all his digitalis pills for his heart first thing in the morning so he would not have to worry about taking them as prescribed three times a day.

We loved it when Grampy came to visit because you never knew what he was going to do. He would spend a few days at our house and then take off for Florida on the bus and be gone for weeks at a time. He chose to spend the Christmas season with us; but when it was time to open gifts, he would not open his because he told us he did not need anything and he would appreciate if we would just store his gifts in an upstairs closet still wrapped and when he needed something, he would open them. I can remember Mother's going to the closet before Christmas and putting his still-wrapped gift from the year before under the tree.

One Christmas season Grampy asked my dad what my mother would like for a gift. Dad thought a minute and said, "You know, she would really like six or eight nice linen napkins for special occasions." A few hours later Grampy called from Freese's Department Store downtown and asked my dad to come get him. My dad thought it a bit strange because Grampy walked everywhere and Freese's was only a little over a mile away from the house; but when he went to pick him up, he understood why he "needed a lift." Grampy had bought my mother napkins, but he had not heard the linen part and had bought her six big cartons of really nice paper napkins. We did not run out of napkins for a long time.

One time Grampy went fishing in the river behind the church and caught a bunch of eels. My mother refused to cook them so Grampy took over. My mother forever banned him from the kitchen after he was done because he left eel skin all over the place when he was finished.

Grampy slept with my brother David in the big bedroom across from my room. Almost every night we would hear Grampy headed for the bathroom in his long johns trying to find his way in the dark. We would hear him fumbling around talking in tongues in a low voice saying things like "teelia, seellia" until he found the bathroom door and would almost shout "Shiloh" with great relief.

My early memories of home were dominated by church, especially when preachers stayed our home. The first guest I remember as a small boy was A. G. Ward, the father of C. M. Ward who would become the famous radio evangelist for 25 years on the Revivaltime broadcast. The thing about A. G. Ward that stood out in my mind as a little boy was the fact that after every evening service he would have a cup of cocoa and then say, "Let's have a good night prayer," so we would all bow our heads and he would say, "Now I lay me down to sleep, I pray the Lord my soul to keep; if I should die before I wake, I pray the Lord my soul to take." Then he would say, "Good night, friends," and totter off to bed. I was really impressed.

One of my favorite guests of all time was Paul Lowenberg. They told me he was a great preacher, but that did not make any difference to me because he was a lot of fun. After devotions every day, he would say, "All right, Charles, it's time to play Crokano"; and we would spend a good hour having him teach me the finer points of a game I learned to love. Indeed, I would later sit spellbound under his ministry. He was to become known as one of the most outstanding orators in the Assemblies of God, a district superintendent, and an executive presbyter. His daughter would marry Dr. James Bradford who served as nine years as the general secretary of the Assemblies of God. Ramona and I would later have the privilege of preaching for him in his church and district.

When I was nine years old, I had a spiritual experience that rivaled my salvation. One Sunday night Dad called the church to the prayer room after his message. Mother told me to wait for her until she was ready to go home. After a period of time, I went over in a corner to wait until she got done praying for a lady. There were very few people left, but the Lord really touched one of our members and he began to sing in the Spirit. I was fascinated because he was a rather quiet guy. All of a sudden out of nowhere I was gripped by the power of God; and for the first time in my life, I began to speak in tongues and then preach in tongues. They tell me I preached in tongues for almost an hour. I remember the message well. I started with Jesus' birth, went all the way through to the ascension, and described the Second Coming and the glories of heaven. I will never know why God chose to save me and fill me with the Holy Spirit in such dramatic ways. I suspect He knew that with my (formerly) quiet personality and the unusual things I would face in the future, I would need those kinds of experiences to keep me anchored and secure, not only to help me but also to minister more effectively in years to come.

In the spring of 1947 came the rather stunning news that my 45-year-old mother was going to have a baby. To say it was a surprise would be an understatement, especially to my dad. My brother David used to love to tell us that Dad said to him soon after the announcement was made: "How do you suppose that happened?"

In October Mother was rushed to the hospital; and in a few hours, my sister Charlotte Ann was born. I was pretty excited. For my first visit to see her, I prepared a very large poster with colorful diamond shape designs with the words "Charlotte Ann, the Princess" in bold letters. I also remember looking out of my mother's hospital room during an evening visit and seeing a bright red glow in the distance. It was the historic fire that almost destroyed the city of Bar Harbor almost 50 miles away including many of the summer homes of the ultrarich.

In summing up my early childhood, like all children, my first conscious memories are fragmented. I am not a trained psychologist, but I believe those memories that stay with us for a lifetime have unintended influence and consequences in shaping what we become. Things happen and words are said to a child that, at the time, are life-changing and all-consuming to that child. To others, they are unimportant and meaningless or frivolous; but to an insecure child (and they all are), they can have a devastating impact to a developing self-image. When the child becomes more adult, it is easy to interpret the past in the context of a mature person. It becomes obvious that many negative experiences of childhood are amusing to recount but what is not obvious is how influential and long lasting they are to the subconscious. We often joke about "puppy love" but fail to realize how important it is to the puppy.

When I was nine years old, my folks decided to take a trip to visit my Uncle Frank Eddy in Detroit, Michigan. My brother and sister were invited to go along, but there was not room for me to go. They tried to explain that the car would be crowded if I went on the trip; and furthermore, they could not afford the cost of the extra bed for hotels or motels. I would be well taken care of while they were gone by a spinster missionary who had agreed to look after me. All the explanations in the world could not ease the fact in my young mind that there was room for my siblings but not for me. It took many years for me to get over that experience and, I am sure, added to my feelings of inferiority and insecurity.

To be transparent, I almost did not mention the above incident for fear the reader would assume my parents were unkind and unfeeling, but nothing could be further from the truth. My purpose was to show that even the best parents in the world can unwittingly underestimate the effect of a decision based on practicalities and not consequences.

In addition to the words and deeds directed toward a child, the whole culture of the home and world as they perceive and mentally define it has an important impact on the rest of their life. I cannot overemphasize the responsibility of parents to create a safe and loving world for the earliest days of a child's life. I was more than fortunate to have parents who did their best to supervise my early life with great love and affection even if some of the rules were unnecessarily strict.

The secular world and now most of the religious world would be very critical of how my parents raised me and even now I disagree with some of their rules and priorities, but any negative was trumped by their ability to prove they always had my best interests at heart to the extent they asked for my forgiveness on several occasions when they felt they had inadvertently hurt me. Indeed, love covers a multitude of sins. I have included these statements about my parents so it could be better understood why they raised me as they did. Very few people have the will to understand because they do not know the context of another person's life. Furthermore, they interpret life and relationships only through the context of their own lives. Most of the time they believe they would have done so much better than those they criticize.

As I was writing this part of my autobiography, I read the results of a special study done by a group of psychologists on behavioral science. The study involved approximately 6,000 older teens. The results were rather surprising. It rather dramatically revealed that those teens raised by parents who were loving but enforced strict rules and discipline were much happier and had a better self-image than those who grew up in a home with few rules and little discipline.

Please pardon my attempt at practical psychology, but the longer I live the more I believe that most of the problems I tried to handle as a pastor grew out of a lack of contextual love (i.e., defining a person by a small number of isolated actions). For the reader to understand my story, it is necessary to understand some of my background.

# CHAPTER 3

**During the summer before going to junior high** school, everything in our family and church changed for the better. Our church had been meeting for several years in a second-floor hall in downtown Bangor. It could seat up to 200 with extra folding chairs on the main floor and 50 in the balcony. Of course, there was no elevator; and I do remember the struggle older people had in climbing the stairs and the chore it was to get Bobby Craig and his wheelchair from the street level to the hall.

It was a memorable Sunday when my father announced to the church that he wanted everyone to pray earnestly about the possibility of purchasing the Husson Mansion on Court Street as a new location. When he stated the purchase price of $22,000, I remember everyone gasped. The decision would be made at a special called church business meeting the following Sunday if my father felt it would be God's will to purchase the property.

During the week following the announcement of buying the mansion, the board met to decide whether to purchase the property. I think it is important for me to digress a bit and tell you things were done quite differently over 70 years ago in the church in which I grew up. First of all, it was an independent Pentecostal church. My father was very suspicious of any "organized religion." He would later become head of the Northern Maine campgrounds and annual camp meeting located at Bridgewater, Maine, used by almost a hundred independent Pentecostal churches in Maine and New Brunswick, Canada. Soon after becoming president, he felt the churches needed a publication to identify cooperating pastors and approved activities and events. He would later decide the youth needed their own camp meeting with a board and committees, but one of his greatest and loudest responses at the camp was when he would say (I heard it several times), "Bless God. We are not all bound up in organization. The Holy Spirit is free to move at this camp." Sometimes more than the Holy Spirit moved, and I will leave that to your imagination.

The legal organization at our church met the bare minimum for a nonprofit. Our board consisted of three officers: my dad as president; my mother as vice president; Evelyn Allen (Mother's closest friend) as secretary; and one member at large, a wonderful black man named Oakley Patterson. The "board" would meet once a year in our dining room. Of course, I eavesdropped on these notable occasions from time to time, and the meetings would go something like this: a brief prayer and the reading of the minutes from the last board meeting followed by the pastor's report which was basically the same every year. "God has really blessed our church this year. Many have been saved and filled with the Holy Ghost, and all the bills are paid. If there are no questions, we will conclude the meeting with prayer; and then I'd like to invite you to stay and have some dessert Helen (his wife, my mom) has prepared."

The annual business meeting of the church was held once a year following the Sunday afternoon service. It consisted of a call to order, prayer, my dad's report which was almost identical to the one given at official board meeting I just described with one addition. I still have a hard time wondering why Dad always insisted the church vote on the pastor every year when it was not necessary. I believe it was an open election because church membership was never mentioned. One year there were two votes against him; and for the next 12 months he wondered aloud from time to time, "I wonder who voted against me?" My brother, sister, and I had about six candidates because we heard stuff our folks never heard; but I must say there was always tremendous unity in the church.

On the Sunday the church voted to buy the Husson Mansion, there was a wonderful confirmation by the Holy Spirit. Someone gave a powerful message in tongues and the interpretation confirming that it was the will of God. When Dad asked for a vote to be taken by a show of hands, he said, "Let the record show there was a unanimous 'yes' vote." There were no "no" votes. As young as I was, I was "blown away" by the praise and rejoicing from that congregation. What happened next will stay with me the rest of my life. People spontaneously began coming to the front, emptying their wallets and purses, and laying their offering on the edge of the platform. Some even gave jewelry and watches. My father later announced that the offering was over $1,000 in cash and sellable items. It is hard for those of us living in the twenty-first century to understand what a large offering that was in practical terms. At that time, the average cost of a new house was $7,700; a new car $1,250; annual wage of $2,950 (a little over a dollar an hour); and a gallon of gas 16 cents.

The renovation on the Husson Mansion began about two months after the epic offering. A friend of my father's who lived in the Boston area offered his services free of charge. Dad gratefully accepted the offer because "Brother Ryan" was a very successful commercial builder. He studied the mansion and decided to open up four rooms on the main floor and create an auditorium seating around 200 people. This he did by inserting steel girders in the ceiling. I cannot tell you how excited our church was on the day we moved from a rented hall to our own building.

The Crabtree family occupied the entire second floor of the mansion plus the kitchen and dining room on the first floor. The house was filled with crystal chandeliers, the two main bathrooms were made of marble from Sienna, Italy—one green and the other a deep pink. The cabinet tops in the large kitchen were covered with stainless steel. David and I occupied the old servants' wing on the second floor which included our own bathroom. Dad had the joy of parking his car in the steam-heated garage in the basement. We were as poor as paupers and lived like kings.

In about two years, the growth of the congregation made it necessary to build another auditorium behind the mansion. The idea of starting multiple services was never a thought for a true Pentecostal church. Those were for Roman Catholics. The decision was made to connect the new auditorium to the back of the "old" church and then open it up to create seating for over 400. The only thing I remember about the actual building of the addition happened when my grandfather who was visiting with us at the time decided he would go ahead with clearing the land for the new building behind the old church while my dad was away on a preaching mission.

He got hold of a carpenter, Billy Washington, to help him cut down the great elm tree which had to be removed. The only problem was that we had not had the plans approved by the city, but these two fine gentlemen ignored that little detail and went ahead and cut down the elm. As if that was not bad enough, Billy was sawing away on a high limb after they felled the tree but did not realize he was cutting the limb on which he was sitting. It was a marvel he did not hurt himself when the limb collapsed and he fell about 12 feet between branches to the ground. I believe the city had mercy on us when Dad went down to the city to confess what had happened on the permit situation.

About the time we completed the new church building, the financial fortunes of our family changed for the better. As previously mentioned, my grandfather Eddy was very wealthy but had practically disowned my mother and aunt after they came into Pentecost. He chose to leave his estate to his sons with the proviso they were to take care of my grandmother until she died. He did leave her a small trust fund as a "safety net." In her will she left my mother and my aunts $5,000 each. To my folks, it was a fortune. My mother, of course, paid the tithe and proceeded to buy all new appliances for the home and some furniture. With the remaining $3,000, they decided to buy their first apartment building because they were "not getting any younger" and, of course, did not own the parsonage.

It would be hard for anyone to imagine the weight of responsibility my father must have felt when he and Mother decided to spend $3,000 on the very first property they had ever bought.

Dad decided to seek the help of the most successful real estate agent in Bangor, Louis Abraham Kirstein. I will leave his religious background to your imagination. Of course, my mother was on "pins and needles" to hear what property her vast estate had purchased.

When my dad came home from his meeting with Mr. Kirstein, he was pretty upset. He reported to my mother that Mr. Kirstein acted pleased to meet him and that he had heard of our church for years. He expressed a desire to really get my folks the best possible deal. After looking at all the possible properties for sale, he told my dad that he had just the rental property to meet their needs. He went on to tell my dad he could probably "pull a few strings" to "sweeten the pot." My dad was immediately conflicted and wanted to know if it would entail being dishonest.

Mr. Kirstein said, "Oh, no, Reverend, just a bit irregular." My dad was infuriated and told Mr. Kirstein, "For you to think I would be party to a dishonest or, as you put it, 'irregular business deal' is offensive. Furthermore, I will never do business with you again." Dad said he was so upset he stomped out of the office without saying goodbye. I will never forget the look of admiration my mother gave my dad. She said, "You did good, Clifford." They were able to find a very nice rental property with three apartment units. My brother and I soon learned that we would become the official wallpaper hangers and painters for that rental and others they would buy.

Several years after my folks bought their first income property, my father received a call from the most unlikely person, Louis Kirstein. According to Dad, the conversation went something like this: "Reverend, I know we've had our differences and I was wrong to offend you, but I just returned from the Lahey Clinic in Boston and they have told me I have a fast-moving cancer. I have a very few weeks to live, and I was wondering if you would be willing to say a prayer for me." My dad told him he would do better than that and would count it a privilege to come to his home and pray with him. I often say now that Mr. Kirstein and Dad are in heaven having a great time appraising property.

A few years after buying our first rental property, my mother heard about a nursing home a few blocks from our parsonage that was up for sale. Mother told Dad she felt strongly she should take a look at it with the possibility of buying it. When Dad asked her who would operate it, she said, "Me, of course. Don't worry, I won't let it interfere with our ministry." To make a long story short, she did buy it, hired a good staff, and owned it for several years. She kept in touch by phone and very seldom visited the home. I remember painting the whole outside one summer for one dollar an hour.

My "career" at high school was quite unremarkable because I was not allowed to be involved in any extra-curricular activities. It is a bit amusing in my mind that the first organized sports event I ever saw was in bible college. One time I did go out for track because I could really run and was doing rather well until I saw a reporter from the Bangor Daily News preparing to do a story on the team. To my horror, I noticed a photographer with him so I used my training in track to run as fast as I could to the locker room to change. I could not imagine the scandal at church if they saw the pastor's son in the sports section. I did listen to the Boston Red Sox games on the sly from time to time.

My only goal in high school was to get through with as little study as possible. I was absolutely delighted to get C's. I would take my homework assignments and textbooks home and proceed to place them on top of the refrigerator. I would leave them there until I would grab them the next morning on the way back to school. They sat there Saturday and Sunday waiting for their walk back to school on Monday. Finally, my mother insisted I leave the books at school if I was not going to use them because they were just cluttering up the kitchen. I still marvel I graduated at 17.

My high school at the time offered a vocational track for boys planning to go into some kind of trade and girls who planned to be homemakers. The other track was for those planning to go to college. I took the professional track for two reasons, the first being the fact that my older siblings had taken it and I was expected to follow in their footsteps. The second reason was the fact that in spite of my total lack of interest in study, I desired to be a medical doctor or, at the worst, in the military medical corps. I very much enjoyed my years in ROTC in high school and thought if I would not be able to go to medical school because of my mediocre grades, I might be able to enlist in the army and become a medic. It was required at that time for every boy to take one year of ROTC. The second and third years required written permission from a parent or guardian. Because I knew Dad would never approve, I forged his name for two years and graduated from the program with the rank of major. I still smile at how detached my folks were from my school life. Into my third year in ROTC, my dad did say, "Charles, it seems to me you are involved in ROTC a lot longer than your brother." (David only took the required one year). He never did know I forged his name. Another thing my folks did not know was that I joined the chess club. They did take note I seemed to be over an hour late getting home from school every Thursday. (Ignorance is bliss).

The college track in high school required foreign language courses. I will never forget my introduction to Latin. We were all a bit early for class on the first day and chattering away when the teacher walked in and proceeded to say in a rather loud voice, "You kids sit down and shut up." The first thought that crossed my mind when I saw her was that she had the longest nose I had ever seen. When I opened my textbook, someone had scrawled these immortal words on the fly leaf. "Latin is a dead language, as dead as dead can be. It killed the ancient Romans, and now it's killing me."

As mentioned previously, I never studied for tests at home. My total disinterest in making decent grades finally caught up with me my senior year. I was in danger of flunking my third year of Spanish which would have been enough to keep me from graduating. My sister-in-law, Dawn, was visiting from Canada. She sat me down and forced me to complete my assignments and made me study for my final. I will always be grateful. It really would have been embarrassing to have flunked my senior year.

In spite of what many would call an abnormal family and church life, I seemed to have a normal attraction and affection for the opposite sex. Of course, I had to be quite careful and secretive; but I did manage to have informal dates such as walking downtown (which took about 15 minutes) with a group of kids between church services on Sunday to have some pizza or Chinese food. During those times, we were able to pair off and enjoy an informal date. It became quite serious when I would "pick up the tab" for the girl I liked. Every summer I would spend two or three weeks in St. John with the Davis sisters. When I got into my teens, I would take the train. They had some really cute girls in the church, and I really liked Barbara. For some time, we kept up a correspondence; and then on her own, she decided to come visit me in Bangor and stay with friends. I was in a terrible bind because I was dating another girl in our church and I knew when the girls found out about each other, my love life would be in the tank. Of course, it happened; and I was without a girlfriend for several weeks.

When I got my driver's license, my love life took a good turn. I really fell for a girl named Beverly Guptill, and we dated for about a year before I went to bible school. Our relationship got into real trouble when one of the saints told my folks they saw Bev sitting awfully close to me while I was driving. We have remained friends for over 60 years. Ramona and I have visited Bev and her husband on occasion. At this writing, they live just outside Bangor.

It would be difficult for people to understand how delighted I was to be able to drive. It was an element of freedom I had never known. I could not only go on dates but also sneak up to Old Town and go to a movie.

In addition, I was able to drive to a wonderful dairy on the edge of town and buy a glass of the best chocolate milk in the world for 5 cents and then all the milk you could drink for 10. My dad used to brag about what a good and careful driver I was. What he did not know was that I would drive carefully out of our yard, go down the street for several blocks, and then peel out. In the middle of the winter, I would take the car down to Green Lake which was frozen over with very thick layers of ice and do "wheelies" and spins. It was great fun.

My growing up years through my middle teens were, on the whole, almost completely dominated by the church. I was never allowed to let school interfere with my church attendance. I do not remember ever missing for sickness. Allow me to take you through a normal church week.

Sunday School started at 1:30 in the afternoon and lasted until 2:20. For the life of me, I cannot remember much at all about Sunday School. In my early years, I do remember teachers using flannel graphs to bring bible stories to life. I do remember the boys' teen class. It met in the furnace room with an average attendance of 5 or 6 and was taught by a candidate for the world's finest monotone voice which was used to articulate advanced theological concepts with no practical application. It was in that class I learned the fine art of daydreaming while looking attentive.

My mother was the Sunday School superintendent as well as the teacher of the large adult bible class which ran an average of over 100. She was a wonderful teacher and preacher in her own right. She would not preach when Dad was in town so I was often asked quite regularly when my father would be away. She was recognized in the northeastern United States as a Sunday School expert; and though she was not Assemblies of God, she was asked to speak at Sunday School conventions and one time traveled to Springfield, Missouri, to participate in a national Sunday School convention. I later learned that many Assemblies of God churches had greater attendance in their Sunday Schools than in their Sunday morning church services.

Every year we had a giant Sunday School contest with another church close to our size in the northeast and several times with St. John when my brother became an assistant pastor there with the Davis sisters. The Sunday School was divided up between the red and blue teams, and great prizes were given to those who brought the most to Sunday School. Dad put up with it because during the six-week contest, the crowds were the largest and many people came to Christ. The single social event of the year was the annual Sunday School picnic where the winning team was honored.

Mother was a true spiritual guardian of her Sunday School and insisted on Assemblies of God curriculum from beginners through adults taught by Spirit-filled teachers. One time she came to my father and told him they would have to relieve a teacher of his class because God had shown her with clarity and great detail he was having an adulterous relationship. Dad told me when they went to the house to confront the man, he said to mother, "God showed you, so you do the talking." When the man came to the door, he greeted my folks warmly and invited them in.

Mother told him they did not need to come in because they had come to get his teacher's quarterly. Of course, the man was shocked and wanted to know why. My mother said, "You know why—because you are living in adultery." The man said, "That is a lie!" My mother said, "You are not lying to us; you are lying to the Holy Ghost!" and proceeded to tell him that God had shown her that the last time he was with the woman, they met in a Boston hotel a week before. My dad said the man acted like he had been "polar-axed." My brother and I often said we dared not sin within 50 miles of Mama. She was powerful.

The main service of the week was at 2:30 on Sunday afternoon. It was pretty exciting because the place was usually packed. Our services opened with a very long song service which consisted of three hymns out of the hymnbook led by a man who only knew one speed— faster. For some reason, if the hymn had four verses, he always omitted the third. I never understood that.

We were never asked to stand when we sang hymns. I kind of agree with my friend, Dan Betzer, who chose as his text one year, "He (Jesus) commanded the people to sit down." Then would come the choruses which averaged three, and we would sing until at least one of them "struck fire." The orchestra always played the offertory (no rehearsal needed). Then we would have announcements which were very brief followed by one or two specials. My brother, accompanied by my sister on the piano, would often play a trombone solo or I would play a marimba solo. Dad would then preach followed by an altar appeal. While the benediction was given, Dad would slip to the back door to greet the people on the way out. It was then he would get the "God-bless-you offering" from many people. He would slip the money into his coat pocket; and after church, he would go to his office in the parsonage (very few churches had an office), take $100 (if that much came in for his weekly salary), and put the rest aside for the missions fund.

At 6:30 every Sunday night, there was a youth service which, of course, the pastor's kids were expected to attend. One of the only services I remember was the time I sang a solo called "The Haven of Rest" without accompaniment, as I remember. To my amazement, the kids began to really worship and praise the Lord. One of the kids got the baptism. It caused such a stir they asked me to sing it in the big service upstairs. As you would suspect, nothing happened. They did not realize that "The Haven of Rest" was too "cutting edge" for adults.

The Sunday night service began at 8 o'clock until David and Hazel started high school. Dad thought they needed to get to bed at a "decent" hour so he changed it to 7:30. We heard from a few people that he had strayed a bit from true Pentecost because he allowed the world to influence the church. The service was almost identical to the Sunday afternoon service with the exception there seemed to be more manifestations of the Spirit such as tongues and interpretation, dancing in the Spirit, and some testimonies. Dad gave a little shorter sermon, and we always had a much longer altar service at the end. That is when people prayed for the infilling of the Spirit and divine healing. It was common to anoint handkerchiefs for people to take to those sick at home or in the hospitals.

The Tuesday night service was the one I dreaded the most. It was called "Testimony Night."

It started with the obligatory song service with no orchestra, just piano and organ. Then came prayer followed by a time for testimonies which lasted a very long time because everyone in the place was expected to testify. I got good at memorizing about ten of them. It was easy because they always said, "I thank the Lord for saving me, and I want to go all the way through with Him." Once in a while we heard a wonderful testimony of healing or answer to prayer. My father ended the service with a brief sermon based on an old outline he had pulled out from a carton he kept by his desk. I had watched him from time to time after supper on Tuesday nights rummaging around until he found one he thought would "bless the people." The service was surprisingly well attended except for young people who had to go to school the next day. The pastor's kids were praised for their faithfulness. They did not know that by the time I came along the idea of skipping a service was never given a chance to be voiced within hearing distance of my parents. That did not keep me from fantasizing about removing Tuesday nights from the church calendar.

The Friday night service rivaled the Sunday night service in attendance and content. I look back in amazement how many people faithfully attended four weekly services and Sunday School.

In addition to our regular services, we always had two or three major revival meetings with a wide variety of evangelists. Most of the time the meetings ran for two weeks over three Sundays. My personal favorite was a Jewish evangelist named Arthur Arnold who held us at least three campaigns. One of his most famous sermons was "Riding the King's Mule." In those days we had the most cutting-edge recording equipment in the world: a wire recorder. A spool of wire was put in the left side on top of the recorder and then hooked up to an empty spool on the right. It allowed for about an hour of recording. I have never been good with mechanical stuff and succeeded in getting the wire all tangled up and ruined the recording. I do not think Dad ever could forgive me, though he tried from time to time.

Between revival meetings, we had many special guests. Dad's two friends who drove to Georgia from Maine with him when they were young became missionaries to Africa for many years. They always visited our church when they were on furlough. The first couple of times they brought slides was kind of interesting; but after a while, I got tired of seeing their missions compounds, groups of natives, and elephants. They ministered in two African countries, but their slideshows and trinkets all looked the same.

Because Zion Bible Institute was less than 300 miles away, we had the presidents, faculty, and choir from time to time. One time we had the choir from Central Bible

Institute clear from Springfield, Missouri. I was really fascinated by one of the girls, not because of her looks but because she was featured as a whistling soloist. You read it right; her expertise was whistling.

One time we were all taken aback when Dad cooperated with a citywide campaign featuring a famous Baptist evangelist, Hyman Appleman. To further shock us, he invited the same evangelist to preach in our 2:30 Sunday service. I remember Dad receiving a lot of criticism for having a Baptist preach in a Pentecostal church. It was a great event.

Six days a week we had what was called "family altar." It consisted of Dad's reading a chapter from the Bible without comment followed by every child saying a prayer, starting with the youngest, which was I for 15 years, followed by Hazel and David. When the children were in school, my mother had her own devotions; but the rest of the time she participated and followed my brother in prayer. Dad ended the family altar with prayer. The family altar was extremely boring overall for the children for two reasons. We were not mature enough to make any application of the scripture to our own lives, especially a great deal of the Old Testament; and it was an almost meaningless routine we had to get through before we could get on with normal living. In raising my own family, I went to the other extreme and did not have regular family altars because I wanted to spare my children what I felt was a discipline of religion and not a part of spiritual life. If I had to do it over again, I would have used family altar as a chance to read a short portion of scripture and discuss it with a view to making a practical application to their lives. I would then ask if they had wanted us to pray about something going on in their lives or in the lives of people they knew. I would then ask the one making the request to pray and we would agree.

It is difficult to criticize my parents in any way because they not only loved God but loved us as well and raised us in the context of a preacher's home. In other words, they were our pastors as well as our parents. Our parsonage was more or less an extension of the church. For instance, most weddings were performed in our living room. I witnessed quite a few of them. One of the most memorable weddings in the parsonage was when an older couple was getting married and the groom was pretty deaf. When Dad said, "Will you have this woman to be your lawfully wedded wife?" the groom looked at Dad with no comprehension. Dad repeated the question in a louder voice, again with no response. In total frustration Dad finally yelled "Well, will you?" to which the groom said, "Yep! Yep!"

Sometimes the roles between church life and home life seemed a bit confusing. For instance, when we questioned Dad about people in the church or why we did things the way we did in our family, he would become rather defensive and think we were questioning his leadership as a pastor, especially if he did not have an answer. Of course, in those days, kids did not dare challenge their parents on any subject so I learned to cope by quietly doing my best to answer my own questions in the context of my own perspective. I got in real trouble one time when my dad said the famous words, "Young man, when I was your age . . .," and I came back with "but when Teddy Roosevelt was your age, he was president of the United States." Let's just say my father was not amused.

For some reason I always hated tambourines in church. Maybe it was because it did not take much training to bang away on the thing. (I refused to call it an instrument.) There were times when we had as many as three of them going which irritated me to no end. One of the sisters insisted on playing hers during every service and did she ever put on a show, shaking it in the air and playing it off her elbows. My brother did not like it either so after one Sunday afternoon service when no one was around, we took the thing and threw it in the furnace. We then helped her look for it before the evening service but could not find it. We had a few weeks of relief before she got another one. Dad kept wondering what had happened to it until he cleaned out the furnace in late spring and found the round metal cylinders. I think he knew who did it but decided not to make an issue of it because he may have not liked tambourines himself.

It may surprise many to know that in our church most of the public services were not distinctly Pentecostal. We would have a message in tongues and interpretation on the average of twice a month, but many evangelicals would have been comfortable attending a "normal service" at Bangor Pentecostal Assembly. About once a month during a Sunday afternoon or evening service, we would have what was referred to by many as a real "gully washer" with lots of singing, a couple of messages in tongues and interpretations, and dancing in the Spirit. When this happened, Dad usually would not preach but end the service by calling everyone to the altar to seek God until they were done. There was no formal benediction. These were the kind of services that drew so much criticism from non-Pentecostals because a lot happened out of the ordinary. I remember one time a lady we called "Sister Bertha" began to dance most vigorously near a heating grate in the floor, put her foot down too hard, and broke the grate with a rather loud crack. Her foot came out quite smoothly, but her shoe stayed stuck in the middle of the grate. The whole incident kind of quenched the Spirit. One of our men yanked the shoe out of the grate but broke the heel. A folding chair was quickly placed over the broken grate for the rest of the service, but it sure was fun to watch how many people avoided that isle. My father loved the moving of the Spirit and even allowed for some of the moving in the flesh, but his patience ran out one day when a visitor was supposedly slain in the Spirit and began to roll on the floor. I've seldom seen my dad so angry. He signaled for a couple of men near our visiting "Holy Roller" and said to one of them, "Get that fellow out of here now." I do not think the guy ever came back.

One rather humorous incident has stayed with me for over 60 years. Because of the normally cool weather in Maine, very few churches had air conditioning. Once in a while, we would have some hot summer days; and since our largest crowds were on Sunday afternoon, the auditorium would become almost insufferable. At such times my dad would say, "Let us all stand and change the air." That was the signal for the ushers to raise all the windows. After the windows were raised one Sunday, Dad said, "You may be seated." As we did, one of the older men sitting behind my grandfather and me passed gas quite loudly. I am still amazed at how well the congregation reacted with hardly a snicker; but my grandfather did turn and say in a rather loud whisper, "Ya did well, Cyrus." I still get tickled thinking about it. That memory came flooding back years later one rather warm Sunday morning at Central Assembly in Springfield, Missouri, when a rather portly usher tried to open a window and caught his pant buckle on the sill, resulting in his pants falling to the floor and exposing some really loud and colorful boxer shorts. As I understand, the poor man never came back to Central.

We did have some interesting preachers stay in our home while they were ministering in our church. Most of them were a joy, others were a bit difficult, and a few were downright odd. One guy was absolutely thrilled with his first electric razor. That was all fine and dandy, but he insisted on using it in his car. To use it, he had to have the engine running which, in my mind, was a bit unnecessary;

but when he insisted in going out to shave in a snowstorm, even my dad thought he was beyond peculiar.

When asked to say the blessing over our dinner, one "odd duck" decided to impress my parents, I am sure, with his spirituality. He stood to say the blessing and proceeded to begin a praise service and talk in tongues for the longest. I was neither impressed nor blessed. My only thought was to wish he would sit down and shut up so I could eat before my food got cold. My parents did not say anything, but I did note he was never asked to say the blessing again while he was with us.

We had one evangelist who decided to fast for three days while he was with us. On the third night, he decided to break his fast and asked Mother for two pieces of toast and two hard-boiled eggs. In the middle of the night, my dad told me he heard him in the guest bathroom gagging and throwing up, obviously quite sick. Dad heard him through the door praying between gags saying, "Come out of me, you unclean devil!" Dad said he could not resist telling the preacher in a rather loud voice in order to be heard through the closed door, "Brother, that's not an unclean devil but those two hard-boiled eggs."

My mom was a very gracious hostess and enjoyed serving most of our guest preachers. I can count on one hand the few she really disliked. One of them was a rather pompous, proud man whom I believe thought he had done us all a favor for being willing to come to our church. He was constantly telling us about the really big churches where he had held wildly successful meetings and the really important people he knew. One morning Mother decided to feed him her famous waffles topped with pure maple syrup. As our guest started to eat, he jumped up and ran to the bathroom next to the kitchen. We heard him in there trying to wash his mouth out, gagging the whole time. Come to find out, Mother had "supposedly" confused the syrup can with a varnish can (we had a hard time believing her excuse). The evangelist tried to wash his mouth out, but he used cold water and the varnish congealed in his mouth. I never will know if it affected his preaching because I did not pay any attention to him because I did not like him.

One of my favorite guests was William Booth Cliborn, the grandson of General Booth, the founder of the Salvation Army. In my estimation, he was one of the best preachers I ever heard. One of his famous sermons on David and Goliath took right at two hours. I was spellbound to the point I was disappointed when he was finished; it seemed like a few minutes. He was a great violinist and was known for packing out Royal Albert Hall in London, England, every year for his special Christmas program for kids. He was also a well-known songwriter. He wrote the beautiful and popular hymn, "Down from His Glory," sung for many years in most Pentecostal churches. The lyrics are magnificent: "Down from His glory, ever living story, my God and Savior came and Jesus was His name. Born in a manger, to His own a stranger, a man of sorrow, tears and agony. Oh how I love Him, how I adore Him, my breath, my sunshine, my all in all. The great Creator became my Savior and all God's fullness dwelleth in Him."

Booth Cliborn was a bit eccentric and unusual. When he was with us, I was 15 years old and was designated his "official" chauffeur. It was in the middle of the summer, and he asked me almost every day to drive him to Green Lake which was about 20 miles from the house so he could swim. What was a bit unusual was the fact he would put on a big straw hat, swim out to the middle of the lake, and just float out there for about a half hour. On the way home he would take a nap. My dad's car was a Lincoln with the first power windows. Cliborn requested every time I would pass a truck or vice versa to put up the window next to him so as not to disturb his rest. When he got back to the parsonage, he would invariably take his shoes off in the living room and dump a bit of sand on the rug. Mother found him a bit of a challenge. One morning he came downstairs for breakfast, and Mother asked him what he wanted to eat. He said, "Sis. Crabtree, I'm not feeling myself this morning so I would ask you to just fix me four pieces of toast and six soft-poached eggs." When my dad gave a bit of a grunt of surprise, Cliborn said, "Aren't you used to feeding real men around here?" I nearly broke out in a cheer when Dad said, "We're used to feeding real men, but we are not used to filling silos." Chalk one up for Dad.

Another great orator we hosted from time to time was Dr. Leonard Heroo who would later serve as president of Zion Bible Institute in East Providence, Rhode Island (the same school I would later serve as president). I will never forget the first time I ever heard him. I was about six years old and can still remember his powerful description of the resurrection of Christ. He was later one of the speakers at the 1958 World Pentecostal Conference held in Winnepeg, Canada. One of his idiosyncrasies drove my dad a bit over the edge. Nearly every time it was time for church, my dad would knock on his bedroom door. Leonard would come to the door and say something like, "I don't believe I have the message for tonight. I am not completely prepared. Your people deserve better." After a period of time and special prayer, Dad would convince him he "was ready." Heroo then would "preach the house down." Dad would ask him to come every year about the same time, but he often would agree to come and then cancel at the last minute. It came to the point Dad decided it was not worth the frustration to disappoint the church so he chose not to invite him again.

It always fascinated me that there were two very good restaurants in Bangor that refused to serve Leonard Heroo because he was black. Leonard, very handsome, carried himself with great dignity and dressed "to the hilt."

My dad told me that Leonard did not seem the least bit put off by the obvious display of racism and would simply say, "I am certain there are other fine restaurants in Bangor that will serve us"; and there were. In our church, I never caught a whiff of racism. There was a very small black population in our city, but two black families were very prominent in our church for many years as well as Oakley Paterson who served on our board.

When I was 13, my brother David and my sister Hazel enrolled in Central Bible Institute in Springfield, Missouri, to prepare for ministry. I had absolutely no intention of following in their footsteps because I had no desire what-soever to be a preacher. It was understood for a long time that David was called to preach and Hazel would marry a preacher. Watching my dad operate as a poorly paid pastor turned me off completely. I dreamed of being involved someway in the medical field, but all that changed one night.

As I have already mentioned, Tuesday night testimony service was the one I really disliked the most for many reasons; but it was incumbent upon me to be faithful. At the end of each service, I was expected to spend some time in prayer. I would keep my "prayer time" to around two minutes. I used to call it my rosary. On this particular Tuesday night which turned out to be as boring as any, I made my way to the altar to please my folks and avoid the questioning of the saints as to my salvation. About a minute into my prayer, God thundered into my spirit these incredible words: "Tonight I am calling you to the full-time gospel ministry." It was so clear, so divine that I knew I was doomed. My response was a rather loud and spontaneous "NO!" which caused more excitement than anything that had happened in that service and set the course for the rest of my life. After that dramatic incident, plans began for me to follow in the footsteps of my brother and sister. I enrolled in Central Bible Institute for the fall semester of 1955. I was 17 years old.

Very few people in the world have experienced the number of miracles I have seen—the clear, supernatural guidance of God—and met so many of the unique personalities in early twentieth century Pentecostalism in the first 17 years of their lives. I am the first one to admit I cannot begin to understand most of it, but I am truly humbled by all of it. In the natural or even in the religious world, I was the least likely and qualified person to be chosen by the unmistakable sovereignty of God to preach the gospel to thousands, pastor two great churches, fill the second top executive office in the largest Pentecostal denomination in the world for 14 years, and end my official ministerial career as the president of a bible college founded by the woman who had knelt in front of me when I was a shy little boy of seven and eight and told me to get ready to be a man of God He could use for His glory.

# CHAPTER 4

My college career began with little fanfare and some problems. I bummed a ride from Bangor, Maine, to Springfield, Missouri, with two guys from northern Maine who were finishing their last year at Central Bible Institute. The distance was approximately 1,600 miles, and we drove it nonstop because we could not afford to stay in motels. I can remember being so tired during one of my driving assignments in the early morning hours that I would drive for a period of time with my window open and stick my head out the window to stay conscious.

When we arrived at CBI rather late morning, I immediately went to the registrar's office to get my room assignment (my dad had already paid the hefty sum of $500 for the semester for my room, board, and classes) and claim my trunk that had been sent by rail because there was not enough room in the car we drove from Bangor. (For some strange reason, the guys I rode with had pretty well taken all the space in their car for their own clothes and necessities.) My trunk had been sent from home a week earlier; but to my dismay, I was informed it would arrive a day or two late because of some unexpected delay.

My first day at CBI was less than wonderful. I was totally exhausted from helping drive for over 40 hours straight; my trunk was late; my roommate had not arrived; and my dorm room was totally bare with no sheets, blankets, or towels. I crawled up on the top bunk with my face to the wall feeling homesick and sorry for myself. It was awful. A few minutes into my "pity party," I said to myself something like, "Just look at yourself. You're acting like a baby. Nobody feels sorry for you, and nobody really cares if your trunk never gets here. Now get up and start acting like a man. Start making some friends. You're going to live here for three years so you might as well make the best of it." So help me, I jumped out of my bunk and went down to the lobby and started introducing myself as people arrived. From that day on, I was really never homesick or depressed. I learned the truth of the scripture: "A man *who has* friends must himself be friendly" (Proverbs 18:24 NKJV).

My first roommate was R. A. McClure, Jr., from North Kansas City, Missouri, where his father was the pastor of First Assembly of God. His sister Dawn had married my brother David the year before; but at the time, R. A. and I had never met. Neither of us knew our families would be intertwined in many ways for the rest of our lives. I soon learned R. A. was delightful but complex.

He was very bright and a very fine singer. He really had no desire to be in bible college and would have preferred to have had a career in musical theater. Like many pastors' sons in those days, it was expected of them to spend at least a year in a bible school to determine God's will for the rest of their lives. In many ways, that was a good thing for most; but I would learn that there were many who were "called to preach" by their parents and not by the Lord. They spent three or four years in a bible school or in some cases went on through seminary and then tried to pastor or be in some other form of full-time ministry—only to fail. I will never forget a pastor intro-ducing me to one of his board members who was recog-nized as one of the finest furniture craftsmen in the state. This board member told me that his father "called" him to be a preacher and, not wanting to disappoint him, he went through bible college and tried to pastor for three or four years. He said he woke up one day to the fact he loved to make furniture but hated pastoring. He deter-mined on the spot not only to become the best possible furniture craftsman but also to become the best possible layman in the Assemblies of God. The pastor told me in his presence that he had accomplished both goals and what a blessing he was to the church. I will always be thankful the call of God was so clear. There would be days I wished I was not a pastor, but I learned that the worst day in the will of God far exceeded the best day out of the will of God.

R. A. would attend CBI for only one year and later go on to pursue a career with Merrill Lynch in New York, but I will say he made the best of the year he spent at CBI and I benefited personally because we would do some good things together.

My normal day at CBI started with a couple of classes. I tried to eat breakfast on the first day and never went back. The big daily event was chapel held late morning. We were assigned chapel seats, men on one side and women on the other in alphabetical order according to classes. To my surprise, my "seatmate" was Robert (Bob) Crabtree, no relation. He would later become a missionary in Europe; president of the Assemblies of God Bible Col-lege in Brussels, Belgium; and later the district superin-tendent of Ohio. He was a joy. His wife, Roberta, some-times gets complimented for my wife Ramona's piano playing. She told me she used to try to tell people she did not play the piano, but it got to the place she simply accepted the compliment and went on her way.

It is embarrassing for me to admit I remember only a handful of the approximately 300 chapel speakers I heard while at bible school. Because we were situated close to the national headquarters of the Assemblies of God, we heard most of the officials as well as many missionaries from time to time plus our faculty. I do remember with quite clarity when Dr. Erickson, a member of our faculty, brushed his notes off the pulpit. They fell on the main floor below the pulpit under the communion table. For the life of me, I do not know why someone near the front did not retrieve them for him but instead we watched with great amusement as he came off the platform and proceeded to crawl under the table to retrieve them himself. He should have realized it was all over as far as anyone listening, but he soldiered on to the end.

A few months into my first year, I went through a profound personal spiritual crisis. Our church in Bangor had become the largest Pentecostal church in Maine running between 300-400 in average attendance, a little above average by today's standards but very strong for the comparatively new Pentecostal movement. Because of that fact, our church drew prominent Pentecostal preachers who stayed in our home. I became well-acquainted with many of them; and when they visited Springfield, several of them invited me to join them for dinner at local restaurants which was to me a welcome change from cafeteria food.

In a period of two weeks, I was invited out to dinner by two well-known preachers. The first was an independent evangelist who had held a two-week revival for my dad a few months before. After the meal, I was shocked to see him pull out a flask and say, "There is nothing better for a Pentecostal preacher than to have a little nip of the right kind of spirits after a good dinner." After recovering from the initial shock, I asked him what would happen if I told on him. With a little wink of the eye he said, "Who do you think they would believe?"

A couple of weeks after my dinner with the "drinker," an AG evangelist who had held meetings for both my roommate's father in North Kansas City and my dad invited both of us to dinner. During the meal, the evangelist said to us, "Let me teach you boys how to raise money when you are on your own. The little old ladies are the easiest touch. Many of them have more money than you think." He proceeded to give us some "pointers" on the right stories to tell and the way to sway an audience emotionally in order to get a good offering.

Sometime between my experiences with the two evangelists, a rather handsome upperclassman with a deep bass voice was "outed" as a homosexual. I hardly knew the term let alone ever met one preparing for ministry.

The three shocking incidents I have just described were too much for me to handle. I began to question whether I wanted to continue preparing for ministry or join the armed forces with an eye to training as a medic and maybe later becoming a full-fledged surgeon. The only thing that gave me pause was the fact that my dad and mom had lived a pure, consistent life both in the church but more importantly in our home. I also remembered my own salvation experience, my dramatic baptism in the Holy Spirit, and the undeniable miracles I had witnessed in my growing-up years. I decided I must get a clear answer to my disillusionment and disappointment. Looking back, I have to smile at what I decided to do. I decided to "give God a night" to show me what I should do with the rest of my life; and if He did not, I would think about dropping out of school.

The night I "gave to God" did not start off so well. I informed the night security guard I was going to spend some time in the chapel praying. I went in a little before 10 o'clock. For about two hours, I sat or knelt in the dark. From time to time I felt like the proverbial idiot sitting, walking, praying out loud, but most of the time just thinking this whole exercise was a waste. Close to midnight I decided to go outside for a few minutes just for a change because what I was doing was not working. It could not have been more than five minutes later standing outside the chapel when I was suddenly overwhelmed by the presence of God, and then He spoke into my spirit. People have asked me from time to time if God speaks in an audible voice. My answer is always the same. "No, He sometimes speaks louder than that; He thunders in the soul." That night He did. Over 60 years later, I can almost remember word-for-word what He said: "You need to know I arranged all of these events of the past few days to teach you that if everybody in the ministry is a fake and if your mother and dad turn out to be hypocrites, your faith is to be centered on Me and not on people; and if you are the only person in the world left staying true to me when I come, I will personally open heaven's doors for you." From that day to this, I have never questioned the faithfulness of God and His Word. Of course, I have been severely disappointed through the years in people and especially in ministers; but I have never been disillusioned about my own salvation, my call to the Pentecostal ministry, and my eternal future.

Soon after that "night with God," I read the story of Madame Guyon, a Catholic saint who went through seven years of religious activities and devotions—never feeling the presence of God. It is hard to imagine faithfully serving God and feeling no emotion. At the end of the seven years, God revealed Himself to her in a very special way and told her that He had withdrawn His presence in order to test her commitment to Him.

God is responsible to us. He has given us all the advice we need. He could not love us more. He could not give us more gifts, but in the end He will not take away our wills. I have watched pastors nearly destroy themselves by living in fear of telling the truth because people might choose to dislike what they hear and leave the church. Others have felt responsible for other peoples' failures or sins. Of course, we are to love people and use wisdom, but we must never blame ourselves for other people's choices. In other words, we are to be responsible to people but not for them. You will ultimately have to answer to God, not people. You cannot do more than to do what you believe in your heart is right in the sight of God. 1 John 3:21 has been an anchor for me spiritually: "If our hearts condemn us not, then have we confidence toward God" (KJV).

During my years at CBI, we experienced two genuine, unusual moves of the Spirit which resulted in classes being suspended for three or four days. Large groups of students stayed all night seeking God. I remember skipping several meals to stay in the chapel. Most of the time it was very quiet. It was as if there was a cloud of God's presence hovering over the chapel and we did not want to leave. Of course, there were times of singing, messages in tongues and interpretations, and kids going to the microphone to confess sin and ask forgiveness. The president or dean was always ready to give a word of exhortation or stop what they thought was pure emotional excess. These special visitations taught me a great deal about true Pentecostal worship, soul searching in prayer, and an appreciation of "all things done decently and in order" (1 Corinthians 14:40 KJV).

Every powerful revival brings out the best and, in some cases, the worst in people. Critics of Pentecost love to point out the excesses and odd behavior in some to discredit any genuine move of the Holy Spirit. Their answer is simply to quickly quench the Spirit and deny any emotional demonstration out of the norm. I watched carefully as wise leadership allowed the moving of the

Spirit and even tolerated some questionable emotional excess until they felt the student needed correction.

Of course, there were some incidents during the revival that the leadership could not anticipate or stop before they happened. For some odd reason one guy got under the grand piano and did some push-ups. I never did learn what the spiritual significance might be in his bit-of-a-confused mind. One young lady went up to the front and tried to speak in tongues in sign language. I will confess I was not spiritual enough at the time to understand one word she signed. One other student testified he spoke in tongues in the Ukulele language. Even the musicians did not understand that one.

The revival was not limited to the main chapel. For many years CBI was the home of the Revivaltime radio broadcast with C. M. Ward as speaker. The choir, under the direction of Cyril McClellan, was made up entirely from the student body. The Revivaltime studio was on the first floor of the women's dorm. During the great revival of which I am describing, many students spent the entire night in that chapel.

In addition to regular chapel services, we had a student-led missionary service every Friday night. Most of the time we heard from senior students who felt a call to missionary service and at other times we listened to guest missionaries. For a time I felt strongly I would become a foreign missionary, but one night I believe the Lord impressed on my heart that I would not be a missionary myself but a promoter and fund-raiser as a pastor to make it possible for missionaries to go to the field.

Once a week just before curfew, we had what was called hall prayers. The men would sit on the floor in their hallway; and the hall monitor, an assistant to the dean of men, would make some announcements, read scripture, give a short devotional, and take prayer requests. The only memorable hall prayer I remember was the time when just before starting, an upper classroom threaded his way through the guys sitting in the corridor toward his room from the shower room totally in the nude. I think he got in some trouble for that, but I am not sure. Thank the Lord I never saw anything like that again.

I do not think there would be many young men 17 years old in these days who would envy my years at bible college: 1600 miles from home, a letter about once a month from my parents, a phone call no more than once a semester, no car, very little money, chapel five days a week, institutional food, classes beginning at 7:30 a.m., curfew at 10 p.m., no single dating, a tiny room with bunk beds for two, and a common bathroom on each hall to service between 40 and 50 male students. In addition, we did not have a radio, phone, or TV in our room.

In spite of what sounds like a very boring existence, we were overall a pretty happy bunch of students. My dorm was a pretty lively place. I well remember a quartet down the hall practicing their music until we had had enough and would tell them in no uncertain terms to "cool it" for a while. They would later become famous in the Assemblies of God as the Courier Quartet and sing together for over 50 years. I would later have them for concerts in both the churches I pastored.

They were outstanding and a lot of fun. They loved to tell about the time when they were doing a concert in a large civic auditorium when one of their members had a terrible urge to run to a bathroom. Fortunately, one of the other quartet members was ready to give the "pitch" for record sales so he took off and made it back just in time for the next song but "announcing" he had just gone to the bathroom by catching a roll of toilet paper in his belt and dragging out the results for all to see.

Eddie Barhum was a good friend who had more money than most of us and drove a new car. On the spur of the moment on a Friday afternoon after classes, four or five of us would pile in his car and drive to Tulsa about 200 miles from Springfield just to have dinner. Most of our outside "dining" took place near downtown Springfield at Big Boy where you could get a huge hamburger and drink for under 50 cents. One time a bunch of us were on a trip, and the 1956 World Series came on. When the national anthem was played, all of us except the driver stood up for the duration. Don Larsen proceeded to pitch the sixth perfect game to that time in World Series history. I remember having to pull over to the side of the road to cheer him on in the ninth inning.

Throughout my three years in CBI, I was always involved in music. Because of my training as a marimbist, I was active in the college orchestra as a percussionist, primarily on the kettle drums. On some selections I played trumpet and was called upon to do solo work in chapel services, primarily on the marimba. During school breaks, the college orchestra would travel to large churches in Missouri and neighboring states to promote the college. The vice president or one of the deans traveled with us as the speaker. My favorite was Dr. C.C. Burnett who was an outstanding preacher in his own right with a great sense of humor. However, there was one thing we could not do. We were absolutely forbidden to even touch his briefcase, let alone move it

One time while he was sleeping in the front seat of the bus, I could not resist taking it and hiding it. When he awakened and reached for his briefcase, there was a bit of a crisis when he did not find it. To make a long story short, I had to confess my theft after he made it clear that everyone on the bus would be punished if the perpetrator did not come forward immediately. Knowing that the kids had seen me steal it, I knew I had no future life or ministry if I did not come clean. When I did, Dr. Burnett ordered the bus stopped and proceeded to order me to ride the rest of the way back to school in the storage bin under the bus. He did not know he had chosen the bin with my trumpet in it, so I dug it out and played it for the rest of trip which was only about a half hour. Dr. Burnett would later preach in First Assembly in Des Moines, Iowa, while I was the pastor. He told me one time that he believed a sermon worth preaching one time was worth preaching 30 times. Sadly, he died quite young from complications of diabetes.

In addition to the choir tours during the school year, I traveled for two summers with a small promotional choir in two ten-passenger vans as a tenor and marimba soloist.

In addition to participating in music, I managed to assemble a large collection of jazz recordings I would play at a very low decibel level in my room. My favorite of all was Erroll Garner (his recording of "Misty"), and Stan Kenton came in a close second. I also collected a number of piano concertos. I tell people that I do not care what they do or sing at my funeral; but if they insist, I would like them to assemble the New York Philharmonic and have Arthur Rubenstein play Rachmaninoff #2 in C Minor.

You may wonder how I could afford this hobby. My father would send me a standard $50 every semester for "extras." Mother would slip a $20 bill in her monthly letter. Every PS said the same thing: "Now don't tell your father about the money." Every semester I would get a letter from Carro Davis with a $10 bill enclosed with a PS which said, "Now don't tell Susie I sent you this money." Susie was more generous than Carro and would slip a $20 bill in her letter each semester with the PS: "Charles dear, please don't tell Carro I sent you this little love gift." You had better believe I did not tell anybody about my very legitimate private "scams."

My preaching "career" began on my first trip home from CBI when I was asked to speak to the youth. I really worked on that first sermon, putting together an outline I thought would take between 20 minutes or even 30 if I got the anointing. Nobody told me how scared I would be, and no one told me I had to say something between every point in the outline. I was able to read the outline and sat down in about three minutes. I never took an outline to the pulpit again. From then on, I wrote out my sermons, did my best to memorize them, and prayed for the anointing. I discovered that was the best way for me to preach.

My preaching began to develop when I joined three other male students as the "pastors" of a little tiny church about 15 miles out of Springfield, housed in what was known as the Washington School House. There could not have been more than 15 to 20 people in attendance on any given Sunday morning. That little group of people must have sat through some very interesting services through the years. I remember asking about a square of newer flooring behind the pulpit. They explained that two years before, a student preacher named Jimmy Brown (who would become quite famous in the Assemblies of God) had stomped so hard one Sunday during his sermon he succeeded in putting his foot through the floor.

Our "salaries" consisted of a free dinner in the homes of two members who alternated Sundays. I remember one Sunday one of the guys had a rather bad cold, and our male host gave him a couple of spoonfuls of what he called cold medicine. He said it was the worst tasting stuff he had ever put in his mouth. Later, one of the guys read on the bottle the words, "for man or beast." It did seem to cure him.

One Sunday, we were privileged to hear a first sermon by one of the team. Out of all the Bible passages from which he could choose, for some reason he chose the subject of circumcision. I have never seen anyone in the pulpit get so confused. After a few minutes of stumbling around the subject, he declared: "You don't have to be circumcised to be saved," and proceeded to sit down. There was quite a sigh of relief for two reasons: Nobody had to be circumcised right away, and nobody had to listen to more of his tortured sermon. I am still thankful for the opportunity to have practiced preaching on such a gospel-hardened and tolerant audience.

At the beginning of my second year at CBI, I met the love of my life. Our introduction was a bit unusual to say the least. My roommate was Jimmy Hearn from Georgia. I believe his greatest contribution to my life was the fact he had a car. (I did not own a car until after I was married). I went with him everywhere, even to Georgia during one fall break to meet his mother. Another benefit of the car was the ability to meet girls at Evangel College which was in its second year of existence. Jimmy became interested in a beautiful young lady at Evangel. At the time, we were not allowed to single date so Jimmy insisted I meet her roommate with the possibility of double dating later. Since I did not have a girlfriend at the time, I agreed—hoping against hope—that her roommate was not too bad looking. As it turned out, Ramona, the roommate, made it about as unappealing as she could. We met her in the laundry room at Evangel where she was tending to her clothes. She was dressed in faded pedal pushers which was bad enough, but she was in the process of giving herself a Toni hair permanent which gave off a rather unpleasant odor. I did not even know she played the piano.

A couple of weeks later, Jimmy coerced me into going with him on a double date. As I remember it, he assured me Ramona was really good-looking under normal circumstances; I had just met her at a bad time. Because I figured I had met her at her worst, I decided for Jimmy's sake I would take another look and am I ever glad I did. We had a really good time.

Ramona's father, Elmo Hudgins, worked for Humble Oil Company (later Exxon), but he was also the president of what was called The Texas/Oklahoma Singing

Convention. Their annual fall convention was a really big deal with a couple of thousand attendees. Quartets such as the Blackwoods and other special groups came from all over the country to participate. The 1956 convention was to be held in Oklahoma City, about 250 miles from Springfield. Ramona was involved so she suggested the four of us all travel in Jimmy's Buick and let her dad foot the bill for our travel and motels.

It was at that convention I learned what a great pianist Ramona was. Between the quartets and special groups, people would lead the crowds in hymns. They needed a piano accompanist (backup tapes and CDs were far in the future), and Ramona was the most popular. I was blown away with her ability; and then when I heard her first piano solo, I could hardly believe my ears. I had grown up with good pianists, but Ramona was in a class by herself.

Ramona and I had a wonderful courtship in spite of the fact we came from two different cultures. My first visit to her home on the outskirts of Pampa, located about 50 miles from Amarillo in the panhandle of Texas, was a new experience. My home life in New England was pretty well regulated by the clock. Dinner right at noon when we were not in school and supper on the dot 5 o'clock and vice versa when any of the family was in school. Mother would ring a bell a few minutes before it was time to sit down. If we missed a meal for any reason, it was our responsibility to find something to eat for ourselves. On my first visit to Pampa, I was up and dressed rather early, ready to sit down with the family for breakfast. I thought there was a bad storm going on outside because the wind was blowing like a hurricane. When I looked out, I was a bit amazed to see Ramona's dad working in his veg-etable garden hoeing way as if everything were normal. In a little bit he came in, got out the frying pan, and pro-ceeded to make himself a hearty breakfast of scrambled eggs and bacon. He sat at the table chatting away while I sat and watched. He did not offer me a bite. When he was finished, he left me alone and rather hungry watching TV and wondering all the time when and if I was going to have breakfast. In a bit, Ramona came in and proceeded to ask me what I would like to eat. I could not get over the family at breakfast in shifts. Schedules were very, very relaxed ("evenin'" was any time after 12 noon). I learned that convenience determined when we ate—not the clock.

Ramona's mom stood about 4'10" and was a delightful personality. She took a while to get my last name straight thinking it was "Crabapple." She got it right eventually, and we had a great relationship until her death. She not only worked hard at home but also became a practical nurse and was one of the most capable and loved members of the staff at the hospital.

When I made my first visit to Pampa, I met Ramona's two sisters, Mackie and Glenna, who were ages four and two, respectively. I often teased Ramona that she was spoiled because she was an only child for 14 years. Maybe one of the reasons we had such a great relationship from the beginning was because I was the youngest in my family for 10 years. We were both spoiled so we understood each other.

Ramona's first introduction to my family took place at the end of the summer just before I was to begin my final year at CBI. Of course, it was a big event. She took her first plane ride and landed in Bangor early Sunday night. I drove her to the parsonage which was next door to the church where my folks were still in service. I cannot imagine the emotions and thoughts of a young Texas gal getting ready to meet perspective in-laws for the first time in the far away land of New England. All went very well, especially when Ramona was asked to play the piano. I always accused my dad of falling in love with Ramona's piano playing before he fell in love with her.

A few days into Ramona's first visit to Bangor, she and I drove to St. John, New Brunswick, Canada, to visit my brother David and his bride of one year, the former Dawn McClure of Kansas City and the sister of R. A., my first roommate at CBI. David was the assistant pastor for the Davis sisters whom my dad had worked with at the beginning of his ministry. We had a wonderful time.

My dad and mom had decided to drive Ramona and me back to Springfield for what turned out to be the last year of college for both of us. Our 1,600-mile journey was a pure pleasure. To save money, we went out of our way a bit to stay with one of my aunts; and to cut down on food costs, we cooked on a portable Coleman stove powered by little cans of fuel we carried in the trunk. I still remember eating steak and all the trimmings surrounded by the Smoky Mountains in a beautiful park.

Near the beginning of Ramona's second year at Evangel, she was asked by her former boss to return to Pampa and work again in the office at the Humble Oil Company. This she did knowing we would probably get married after I graduated and wisely assumed I would begin my ministry with very little money. In February of the following year, she came up one weekend to visit me in Springfield. It was during that visit that I took her to a great restaurant called the Shady Inn to formally pro- pose. Earlier in the day, I took the engagement ring to the restaurant and asked them to bring it to our table in some Jell-O. It is hard to imagine doing such a thing in today's culture. During the meal, I was asked to come to the front on some pretext and was informed the kitchen staff could not stand the ring up in Jell-O and wanted to know if sherbet would be okay. When it came time for dessert, they brought out the sherbet with the ring standing up proudly in the middle. Of course, Ramona was shocked and could not do anything but say "yes" to my proposal. When she did, the whole restaurant broke into applause because the staff had alerted everyone to what was going to happen. We soon set the date for the wedding for November 1,1958, a few days after my twenty-first birthday. I wanted to wait until I could sign my own wedding license.

My old habits as a student in high school continued. I thought that attending classes was enough schooling for one day. I jokingly said, "I'm not going to let my studies interfere with my education." I was happy with a C average. After all, my first and last name began with a C. One required subject I had to take during my first year was entitled "History and Doctrine of the Assemblies of God." On the first day of class our teacher made two mistakes. He told us that we would have three tests based on the textbook and that class attendance was taken by signing in at the door. The first class was so boring that I decided to break my old rule of not studying between classes and proceeded to read the rather short textbook, go to each class long enough to sign my name at the door, and then leave. On test days, I did go to class and take the exam. I aced the course. It was all I could do to keep my composure when the teacher introduced me to someone years later as "one of my best students."

My whole life and future ministry was dramatically changed one day when Dr. Donald Johns, one of my favorite teachers, called me into his office after an ethics class a month into my second year. I was sure I was in some kind of trouble as I stood in front of his desk because he did not ask me to sit down. I will never forget it. He looked me up and down for what seemed a long time, probably only seconds, and then said these immortal words: "Crabtree, I suspect you have a brain; but you're not using it. I'm not happy, and I don't think you are either. Now go on, get out of here, and make a 100 on everything from now on." Of course, I did not; but I came close most of the time. I found study to be a delight. I remember taking 21 semester hours during my final year in addition to playing in the college band, being editor of the college paper, and carrying on a heavy romance while making an "A" average.

In looking back, I always regretted not asking Dr. Johns why he spoke to me at that particular time. I suspected he was impressed by the Holy Spirit to do so because the Lord knew I was ready to receive it. From that time on, I have tried to be very sensitive to when people, especially young people, would be ready to receive a word of encouragement or correction. "A word fitly spoken" (Proverbs 25:11 KJV).

A few years after the Dr. Johns' incident while serving as a young pastor at First Assembly in Des Moines, Iowa, I was shocked to learn that I had been appointed to the World Missions Board of the Assemblies of God. My carnal, suspicious mind reasoned it would not cost them much to bring me from Des Moines to Springfield, Missouri; and a kid preacher around 30 years of age would not give them much trouble. I remember arriving early for the second meeting of the board held in the headquarters building. I was standing looking out the window toward Cox Hospital across the street. I saw an ambulance pull up and later learned the patient was Dr. Johns who had died before he got to the hospital. I decided when I heard the sad news to be more diligent in expressing appreciation to people who had proved to be a blessing to my life or ministry. I will always regret not thanking Dr. Johns for the profound effect he had on my life and ministry.

My three years at CBI turned out to be invaluable. To be honest, the move away from resident bible colleges in the last few decades is, in my opinion, a serious mistake. I know the realities of cost and the trend toward advanced degrees through distance learning are just some of the reasons; but in looking back, I learned more outside of classes to prepare me for ministry than the official curriculum and classroom. No other setting could provide the hours of informal dialogue concerning ministry among peers. It forced me to defend my value system and convictions. No other setting provides the times of daily worship and the concentrated bible study taught by Spirit-filled professors. Add to all of that the joy of having lifelong friendships in ministry which began in dorms and the cafeteria cannot be realized any other way. I would not trade my three years at CBI for anything in this world. In my thinking, "distance education" means just that.

# CHAPTER 5

**The summer after my graduation from CBI and** before my wedding in the coming fall, I received an invitation to be an intern at First Assembly of God in Duncan, Oklahoma. The pastor was Haskell Rogers. My first assignment was to lead the music for Tommy Barnett, a dynamic young evangelist who loved to do illustrated sermons. I will never forget his message: "Road Blocks on the Road to Hell." I believe it was the first illustrated sermon I had ever seen. He had three wooden road barriers like low fences put up on the platform; and after each main point, he jumped one of the barriers and preached another main point. I do not remember if he jumped the last barrier. Years later I would have the joy of preaching at his great church, First Assembly in Phoenix, Arizona, and also at his Dream Center in Los Angeles.

First Assembly in Duncan was considered a good church which averaged around 200 in Sunday morning attendance at the time I was there. Since I was only to be at the church for five months, I was not given any portfolio and very little money. There really was no need or probably inadequate financial resources for the church to have paid staff of any kind. My role that summer was basically to fill in for volunteer staff who were on vacation so I did a little bit of everything from teaching a class, leading the song service, and even preaching a couple of times on Wednesday nights when the pastor was gone.

In putting my experience at Duncan in perspective, I learned some very important lessons I did not know would be valuable at the time. I am still amazed at the genius of God not only in guiding me to the right places at the right time but also in using those places to prepare me for the unknown. I had no idea at the time that in those few weeks God was teaching me how to become better prepared to be a full-time assistant pastor in an Assemblies of God church, my next assignment.

Haskell Rogers was very much an Assemblies of God loyalist. He was extremely involved in his section and would later become the district superintendent of the West Texas District. He taught me by example and observation how much my father had missed both in his personal life and pastoral career by choosing to be independent. To be honest, I do not believe that ministers who grew up attending an Assemblies God church could have the same positive perspective and appreciation I have for being a part of a strong Pentecostal fellowship or denomination. It may sound strange, but I did not consciously learn most of the things I am now going to mention concerning being part of the Assemblies of God until later in my ministry. To put it another way, it is difficult for a person to learn a lot of things in ministry until they go through the "University of Practical Experience." I will mention three important lessons I learned in the few months I spent in Duncan. There would be many more to follow throughout the rest of my ministry.

1.  Although not all, many ministers want to be independent because they do not want to be under spiritual authority. They claim the only authority they

are under is the God of the Assemblies, not the Assemblies of God. Of course, the Bible does not mention any denomination specifically but is very clear about the need for everyone to be answerable and in subjection to recognized spiritual leadership in the body of Christ. That principle is basic even in the secular world where the powers or rulers are ordained of God. We must see authority as a protection and necessity for anybody to function effectively. There are many wonderful "independent" ministers, but the best of them do seek direction and wisdom from other ministers they respect. However, many who want to be independent do not want to be questioned about their doctrine, lifestyle, or any financial accounting. I was very wary of joining the Assemblies of God, but I learned from Haskell Rogers it is an incredible blessing to anyone who believed the fundamental doctrines of scripture and wanted to live above reproach. He taught me that the only time I needed to be afraid of being part of the Assemblies of God ministry is if I did not want to do right or preach false doctrine. I learned through over 50 years of ministry that the Assemblies of God never once hindered my spiritual life or interfered with any God-given goals.

2. One of the things my father did not get to enjoy as an independent minister was the wonderful fellowship many in the Assemblies of God take for granted and that is the serendipity of rich fellowship experienced through the organization on local, sectional, district, and national levels. During my few months in Duncan, I learned to appreciate the camaraderie of a section which consisted of a part of the district with around 20 to 30 churches on average. Haskell Rogers made sure I attended every one of the monthly meetings. He knew how

important it was to form good relationships with those who lived and ministered in relatively close proximity to our local church. Later in my ministry, I learned the importance of fellowship on a district and national level.

3. Another thing too many of us in the Assemblies of God do not appreciate enough are the incredible resources made available. I learned in Duncan that when I pastored, I would have access to great personnel such as national leaders, evangelists, and outstanding teachers. I cannot begin to communicate the value of access to the greatest missions program in the world. In growing up in an independent church, my father only knew two or three foreign missionaries he could have for a missions emphasis. In addition to personnel, the resources offered through the Assemblies of God for children, youth, adults, seniors, music, finance, and a long list of programs and materials are too numerous to mention. I still smile when I think of my growing up years and how proud my father had been that he was not "bound to any denomination." When he wanted to build a great Sunday School, he used Assemblies of God material. When he wanted to have Pentecostal music in his church, we sang out of Assemblies of God hymnals. When he wanted to have revival meetings in his church, he came to the point he would only use Assemblies of God evangelists because he could be sure they would not preach false doctrine and could be trusted in the areas of morals and money. I will never forget one time when Dad decided to have an American Indian who was supposed be an important chief with a great Pentecostal ministry opening new churches on reservations. He came to our church and received one of the great offerings to help

reach the Indians in Arizona. Later we found out he was a total fraud and pocketed all the money for himself.

Of course, the Assemblies of God is not perfect as no organization is; but I am convinced that like Noah's Ark, it is the best thing afloat. I will always be grateful for my experience at First Assembly in Duncan, Oklahoma, as I was able to see firsthand for the first time from the inside how important it was for me to align myself and ministry with a solid organization. I learned that the benefits far outweigh any perceived negatives or criticisms.

At the end of October 1958, my future brother-in-law, Bob Hoskins, came to First Assembly in Duncan for a brief series of meetings after which he accompanied me to Pampa, Texas, in order to participate in my wedding. Neither of us owned a car, so we took the train. I first met Bob when he came to preach for my dad in Bangor, Maine. He and my sister Hazel had met in California, and a romance ensued. Of course, my folks were anxious to meet him; and since he was reputed to be an outstanding preacher, my father invited him to preach at our church in Bangor (a very clever way to meet and have a good look at their daughter's boyfriend). At the age of seven, Bob had an "out-of-body" experience during which time he had a vision of heaven and hell and was told to begin preaching the gospel which he did immediately and became one of the most famous child evangelists in history. He was more than a brief phenomenon and curiosity who not only drew thousands of people to his crusades in America but also at the age of 15 got on a plane and flew to Africa with no contacts and began a truly God-ordained and directed worldwide ministry. I will have to admit I was "blown away" by his preaching. I still remember the first sermon I ever heard him preach entitled "They Went Home Another Way," speaking of the wise men. That was over 60 years ago so you know it had to have been an exceptional sermon.

On November 1, 1958, Charles Talmage Crabtree and Lois Ramona Hudgins were married at First Assembly of God in Pampa, Texas. Officiating was the pastor of the church, J. S. McMullen, and the groom's father, Clifford Crabtree. It was a beautiful, sacred ceremony with approximately 200 in attendance. It was a traditional wedding for the groom until he was informed that he had to push the bride in a wheelbarrow (gown and all) to the reception over a mile away.

It is absolutely imperative that I mention three very large problems I faced in preparing to "take upon myself" a bride. One, I had no money; two, I had no car; and three, I had no job. The first problem was solved a month before my wedding when I received word my Grandmother Eddy had left me $1,000 in her will and the "check was in the mail." It would be like receiving at least $8,000 in today's money. I knew before the wedding that the second problem was also solved. Ramona had left Evangel a year before and had gone to work for Humble Oil Company. During that time, she had purchased a brand new 1957 Ford Fairlane 500 (now a classic). I was confident the third problem would be solved during the honeymoon because I had been asked to interview for two ministry opportunities, one in California as an assistant pastor and the other in Oregon as a youth pastor.

We had one of the most unique and overall fun honeymoons in history. After the reception, we jumped into our Fairlane 500 (I soon learned that the car was not totally paid for so "her" car became "our car") and drove from Pampa to Amarillo—about 50 miles. To our great relief, none of the rumors materialized that we would have our car all decorated and be followed by a bunch of friends who would torment us half the night.

The honeymoon lasted for three weeks, and we enjoyed every minute of it. The only negative I remember was car trouble. We had some engine trouble that cost over $200 which was, in our thinking, astronomical because it ate up almost a quarter of our cash. To add insult to injury, while we were driving through Los Angeles, some mindless idiot threw a Coke bottle under our car and ruined a front tire. Other than problems with our car, we had a memorable honeymoon.

In a period of three weeks, we visited Steamboat Springs, Colorado; Salt Lake City, Utah; Portland, Oregon; San Francisco, Los Angeles, Sacramento and Carmel by the Sea, California; and Las Vegas, Nevada, where on impulse I put a total of three nickels in a slot machine and hit a jackpot of $30. It scared me to death, and I have never "gambled" again. In Salt Lake City, we decided to take a cab to a highly recommended downtown restaurant from our motel because we had no idea where it was. Of course, there was no such thing as an electronic guidance system. A cab ride was so cheap in those days that a parking fee might have been more expensive. We had a great dinner and on the way back to the motel, our cabbie, learning we were on our honeymoon, proceeded to give us a full sightseeing tour of Salt Lake City free of charge. All he accepted was the cost of a cab ride from the restaurant to the motel. The next day we went shopping, and I bought two very fine top coats—one gray and the other brown—for just over $50 total. I wore those coats for years.

To say we lived "high on the hog" during our honeymoon would not be an exaggeration. We ate at the finest restaurants and stayed at world class hotels. For instance, in San Francisco we stayed at the wonderful downtown Sheraton and feasted at LeBouef's where we decided to sin big time and try a Manhattan cocktail. We took one sip and grimaced. The smell and the taste made us wonder how in the world anyone could drink that stuff. We proceeded to top off our stay by attending a live performance of *Mame*. (How's that for a couple of unemployed Pentecostal preachers?)

Allow me to make a rather serious observation in looking back on our honeymoon. We have a tendency to laugh a bit about my "big" jackpot in Las Vegas and our "big single sip drinking binge" in San Francisco because they did not lead to a gambling or alcohol problem that could have destroyed our ministry. I have often wondered what would have happened to me if I had caught the "gambling bug" when I hit the jackpot, as small as it was, or if Ramona and I had really liked the taste of that Manhattan cocktail. The results could have been disastrous. I do not remember dealing with ministers who had a gambling problem although I am sure there are some, but I have seen several very gifted and successful ministers lose everything because of alcoholism. It all started with a first time and then "a little never hurt anyone" or "our church was too legalistic" or "no one will ever know." I learned on that honeymoon that marriage is a wonderful part of God's plan and gives a couple the freedom to live their own lives free of many restraints, but it is also a test. It opens the door to all kinds of new temptations and quite quickly reveals the motivation behind conduct.

It is important for me to point out that I have avoided all kinds of disasters that could have ruined my relationship with God, my wife, and ministry. On the surface it looks like I was just plain lucky in a lot of situations; but upon reflection, I look back and thank God for His protection when I did not even realize it. Was it luck way back when I tried smoking with my cousin and nearly got sick? Was it luck that from day one I could not stand the smell of beer to the point I did not even taste it when "nobody would have known?" Was it luck Ramona and I could not stand the taste of that Manhattan in San Francisco, and was it luck I got a little scared when I hit a small jackpot? I do not think so. I believe God answered the prayers of godly parents and, more importantly, my own prayers to keep me from falling into what would have been sin for me and the terrible consequences. We have often been too quick to criticize the strict rules of conduct demanded by our spiritual fathers, but in most cases they were put in place because they loved God and loved their children and knew all too well the consequences of what some would call "innocent" sins. Consequently, I do not think of myself as a lucky person but as a blessed person whom my God and my parents loved enough to do their best to protect my life, my soul, and my eternal future.

As already mentioned, the main reason we went to the west coast on our honeymoon was to interview at two churches for a ministry position. The first church we visited was First Assembly in Paramount, California, a comparatively small city bordering Long Beach and Compton. Nearly every one of our churches had "Assembly" in the name, and almost without exception the only Assembly in a town or the first one established was named First Assembly. The pastor at Paramount was Ted Singleton. The church ran a little over 200 in attendance, and I was offered a very undefined and open portfolio with the title of assistant pastor with my main responsibility being to youth. Actually, my job could have been defined as anything the pastor wanted me to do. We were offered $65 a week and a small parsonage across the street from the church.

The second church we considered for ministry was First Assembly of God in Eugene, Oregon, pastored by Murray McLees. It was considered a very large church at that time running around 500 in attendance. We had a very good interview. I was offered the position of youth pastor at a salary of around $100 a week plus housing. Unlike Paramount, the position was very well-defined and the pastor was clear as to what my responsibilities would be. For some reason, one statement bothered me. He told me my position did not include any opportunity for preaching. Actually, Pastor Singleton in Paramount did not offer preaching opportunities either, but both Ramona and I felt quite strongly not to accept the position in Eugene and proceeded to call Pastor Singleton to tell him we felt we should return to Paramount if he still wanted us. He told me without hesitation to come back. The next Sunday we were formally introduced to the congregation as their new assistant pastor.

The 18 months we spent in Paramount turned out to be some of the most enjoyable of our lives. The experience was "tailor-made" for raw recruits in the ministry, starting with the pastor and his wife, Ted and Gwen Singleton. From the start, we called them "Big Mama" and "Big Daddy" for obvious reasons. They were both delightful Southerners originally from Arkansas. He was very relaxed and full of fun. She made the best tacos and fried chicken in the world. They had a couple of sons living at home, but we were as much a part of their family as they were. Big Daddy loved baseball, and it was not long before we were big Dodger fans and went to their home games as often as we could. The Dodgers had just moved from Brooklyn and were playing in the Los Angeles Coliseum. We could not afford to go too often because the tickets for a good seat cost $7 which at that time was astronomical. The most memorable game I remember was when we joined 73,000 fans and watched Sandy Koufax strike out a record 21 batters. He started the game by walking the first three batters and then striking out the next three. It was a great team including Don Drysdale, Wally Moon, and Duke Snyder among other notables. They went to the World Series two out of the three years they played in the Coliseum while their new stadium at Chavez Ravine was being built.

Over the months, our ministry at the church grew quite rapidly. Ramona was very active in music. Shortly after getting settled, she became the church pianist and played and arranged for the choir and small groups. (Her men's trio was outstanding). Together one Easter, we decided to write a cantata for the choir. It was well-received but did not become an international "hit." I think we were too far ahead of our time.

For my part, I am still surprised at the varied responsibilities I was given over our time at Paramount. I began as the youth pastor and then led the choir because the former assistant had filled that role. I still do not know how or why I was asked to take charge of the Sunday School, but I really enjoyed it and God blessed our efforts and the average attendance grew from a little over 200 to over 300 in a year. During that time, I made the mistake of taking on my mother in a six-week Sunday School contest. She really humbled me with a huge win. It was one of the few times in history that Maine beat California.

A few weeks into our ministry at Paramount, the teacher of the adult Sunday School class that was held in the main auditorium moved away and I was asked to fill in until another teacher could be found. Looking back, it turned out to be one of the most important assignments in my entire ministry. It was in that adult class I learned to preach. I had preached a handful of times but never on a regular basis. For some strange reason, I decided not to teach the adult class but to preach it. In those days, we used Sunday School quarterlies for every age group including adults. From the first Sunday as the adult Sunday School teacher, I used the quarterly as a sermon outline. I learned in that class how to build a sermon using the subject as a "hidden" foundation, meaning I never strayed from the foundation while developing the message. Sunday by Sunday, I got a little better at the "art" of preaching which is never fully realized; but I became more confident in hearing from God on a subject and articulating truth. Big Mama always attended my class, and sometimes in my youthful exuberance I would begin getting a little too harsh or over the line at which she would catch my eye and then shake her head. Nothing ever caused me to "lose the anointing" quicker than her disapproval. I will always be grateful she was there.

Big Daddy turned me on to a series of books which continues to enrich my life and ministry.

Keswick is an annual convention held in the lake region of England. The first convention was held in 1875, and they are still in operation. Each year, the convention publishes an annual called "The Keswick Week." In my estimation they are the greatest source of Bible teaching and sermons in the world on a consistent basis. The annuals before the 1980s contained two full bible studies plus all of the individual sermons. I have kept close to 100 annuals dating from 1902. They continue to be a source of real inspiration to me.

A close friend of the Singletons was Wesley Goodwin who for some strange reason decided I should share his love for sermon books. He introduced me to some of the great and comparatively little-known preachers of the past. He gave me my first sermon books by such men as A. C. Dixon, J. Wallace Hamilton, Percy Ainsworth, and G. H. Morrison. I not only read all of them but also graded each sermon from AAA to CCC to help me amass the beginnings of a great library which would ultimately grow to around 10,000 volumes after 40 years of acquisitions. While in Paramount, I was made aware of a used book store in the city of Long Beach called Acres of Books. It was less than five miles from my house. They had a wonderful religious section where I would browse about every two weeks and pick up great books for as low as 10 cents. I do not remember ever paying more than 25 cents for any sermon book.

Because of my "preaching" in my Sunday School class, I was asked more and more by Big Daddy to preach on Wednesday nights, Sunday nights, and sometimes even Sunday mornings. I am still amazed at the wisdom of God in directing both Ramona and me to accept Paramount over Eugene. In the natural it would have seemed to be a "no brainer" to take a position in a larger church with a better salary, but the Lord knew I could not have developed my preaching ministry in Eugene and Ramona could not have been used as effectively in music.

After only 18 months at Paramount, God began to put into my mind and spirit a stronger and stronger urging to step out in faith and go on the evangelistic field. It got to the point that I felt if I did not do it, I would find myself out of the will of God. It was a bit unnerving for me to call my dad and explain my conflict. He said, "If you want my advice, I do not believe you should do it. You have a good ministry where you are. The pastor and the people love you, and I can tell you that the evangelistic field is very difficult." I had always honored my dad in matters of ministry; but after prayer, I felt strongly that for the only time in my life I had to go against my earthly father's advice and obey my heavenly Father. I sat down with Big Daddy and told him we would have to leave if I were to stay on track in the will of God. He was disappointed but very gracious. In one month, Ramona and I took that huge step of faith into the unknown with only three meetings scheduled and no money. Our lives would never be the same. I will always be thankful the decision was made difficult because I knew it would have been much easier to stay in a comfort zone of convenience.

The evangelistic field then was far different than it is today. Nearly every church had at least two "special meetings" or "revivals" every year. There was some preaching to the unsaved, but most of the messages in an Assemblies of God church concerned the baptism in the Holy

Spirit, divine healing, faith, sanctification, and prophecy. The person who preached them was called an evangelist because of the fact he or she traveled from church to church and played the role of part prophet, teacher, and evangelist.

The beginning of our three-and-a-half year career on the evangelistic field was about as "bare bones" as you can imagine. We bought a 1960, four-door stick shift Ford with no power anything including air conditioning. Later when we would go through Arizona, we would go at night and roll the windows down to survive the heat.

Our first meeting after leaving Paramount was in Manhattan Beach, California. To say it was a unique situation is an understatement. The church was a designated Home Missions church which simply means the district office served as their legal authority and the pastor was appointed and served at the will of the district officials in consultation with a small local church committee. In the case of the Manhattan Beach church, the pastor supplemented his income as a professional boxing promoter. If you do not think it was difficult to preach to less than 50 people after the pastor introduced you and then went to his office to work on setting up fights on a very loud typewriter, you simply do not get the picture. The next two meetings we held were much better in every way. Of course, any place after Manhattan Beach was comparatively wonderful.

We were advertised as "The Musical Crabtrees" because we started our part of every service with either a piano solo, a marimba or trumpet solo, or a vocal duet. Without question, Ramona's part was best of all. We went "big time" when we produced a 45 record with four of our most requested musical arrangements. We sold them for $1.

Our third meeting took place in Crane, Texas, and stands out in my mind because into the second week we had no more meetings scheduled which, simply put, meant we had no place to go after the coming Sunday. You can imagine my prayer life intensified day by day along with my panic. I had a wife to support, very little money, and a $65 car payment. On the second Thursday, four days before we were scheduled to leave Crane, the pastor handed me the phone and said, "A pastor is asking to speak to you." He introduced himself as Gordon Speed, the pastor of the First Assembly of God in Comanche, Oklahoma, and proceeded to tell me an amazing story. He had been reading the Pentecostal Evangel (the official weekly publication of the Assemblies of God) and was glancing down the list of special meetings in progress across the nation along with the location and name of the church and the names of the pastor and evangelist. The next thing he told me proved to be one of the great miracles of my ministry. He said, "When I saw your name, God clearly said, 'Have him.' I told the Lord I did not know you but would look into it, find out a little about you, and schedule a meeting when it was convenient for both of us." He then told me that the Lord said to him in no uncertain terms, "I know him, and I want you to have him now." Bro Speed then said, "You must be very special. Can you start with us Monday night?" I said, "I don't think I can make it Monday, but we can be there Tuesday." We had a wonderful two-week meeting; and from that time on, we had very few interruptions in our schedule for the next three and a half years.

Our travels took us as far east as St. John, New Brunswick, Canada, where we held a meeting where my brother David was the assistant pastor for Carro and Susie Davis (mentioned earlier in the book); as far north as New Castle, Wyoming; as far south as Texas; and as far west as California.

Looking back over our ministry as evangelists, I am struck by the "sameness" of the local church during the late 50s and early 60s. Nearly every church had Sunday School at 9:45 and used the same curriculum from beginners to adults produced by the Gospel Publishing House in Springfield, Missouri. Sunday School was a "big deal." As visiting evangelists, Ramona and I were expected to attend an adult class either by sitting through one or being a "guest teacher." The worst class we remember attending was when the teacher took his Adult Teachers Quarterly and proceeded to read it word-for-word, including the introduction. He even read, "Roman numeral one, A," etc. He came to the end of reading and said, "Well, Springfield cut it a bit short this week"; and so help me, we sat there for over 10 minutes saying nothing. I used the time to pray for my message. There were some churches who had a larger attendance in Sunday School than in the Sunday morning service. The Sunday School superintendent whom today would be the Christian Education director was a lay person but was considered second only to the pastor in importance. He or she appointed the teachers and, in many cases, held regular teachers' training classes. At 10:45, a bell would ring; and everyone would move to the auditorium where the superintendent would announce the attendance for the day which would have already been posted on the Sunday School board prominently displayed in the lobby giving the attendance for that day, the attendance the prior Sunday, the amount in the Sunday School offering and other pertinent information. As an evangelist, I was always relieved if the attendance was better than the Sunday before because it usually lifted everyone's spirits. Of course, the reverse was true. The superintendent during the pre-service meeting would announce the birthdays, and we would have to sing these lyrics: "A happy birthday to you, a happy birthday to you, may you feel Jesus near, every day of the year. A happy birthday to you, a happy birthday to you, and the best year you've ever had." This would be followed by recognizing everyone who had an anniversary that week, and we would sing the same lyrics as the birthday song, simply substituting the word "anniversary" for the word "birthday." The Sunday School treasurer would often be asked to report on the offering and then step back to let the superintendent finish with a brief promotion and prayer. I still laugh about the poor treasurer who realized his pants were unzipped and decided to remedy the problem by hiding behind the lady superintendent when he finished his report but got the zipper caught in her rather voluminous skirt and proceeded to hop along behind her for a few steps when she had finished her report.

Nearly every Sunday morning service across the nation began by singing two or three hymns out of an Assemblies of God hymnal followed by two or three choruses which often "caught fire" resulting in a rather lengthy time of praise. Then came prayer, announcements, the offering, and the offertory by a robed choir in a big church and a group from the audience called to the front before the song service in a smaller church. This was followed by the sermon. The altar call included an appeal for salvation and often healing.

The differences in Assemblies of God churches when Ramona and I were on the evangelistic field was, of course, in size. The Assemblies of God was not yet 50 years old at that time, and you could count those of 1,000 or more on one hand. However, the greatest difference in churches was not in worship styles, theology, or programs but in the personality, administrative ability, work ethic, and preaching of the pastor.

The idea of trying to do any kind of two-week revival emphasis with services every night between Sundays (except Saturdays) would be almost ludicrous to think about in the 2000s, but indeed the church operated in a very different culture which encouraged faithfulness in attendance for many reasons. When Ramona and I traveled on the evangelistic field, few people had money to travel, build vacation homes, and take more than two weeks out of their work schedule. In addition, there was no TV to speak of. The public school system was very sensitive to the church and never scheduled any sporting events on Sundays. In some areas of the country, there were no special events scheduled on Wednesday night because nearly every evangelical church had Wednesday night Bible studies and special programs for children and youth.

In all the time we traveled on the evangelistic field, I do not remember the church putting us up in a hotel or motel. Most of the time we stayed with the pastor and his family in the parsonage. Many of the churches had what were called "evangelists' quarters" consisting of a couple of rooms in the church building itself. A few times we stayed in the homes of well-to-do members. Overall, our living arrangements were comfortable and clean. One notable exception was in a parsonage which was so dirty that Ramona felt it necessary to put papers down to iron our clothes because of the dog hair all over the house. The pastor's wife sat on the living room couch most of the day staring at the TV. Every afternoon we went over to the church and napped on the platform floor. Luckily, we were there for only one week. Surprisingly, it was a good-sized church and the pastor was the presbyter of the section.

Ramona still uses some of the fabulous recipes she picked up from our hosts who would serve us their specialties. However, she decided not to keep the recipe for grilled chicken which one pastor enjoyed cooking. In that case I suspected he was lying to us when he stated that he "enjoyed chicken a little rare." The Lord gave us the ability to nibble a bit around the edges and not get sick.

It would be impossible to go to so many places, preach in so many churches, and live with so many people and not have many memorable moments—both good and not so good. I have chosen to have mercy on my readers and recount just a few.

Ramona still likes to tell about the first meeting we held in Brooklyn, New York, in an old building directly across the street from the El which would shake the building a bit every time the train would go by and drown out the preacher a bit. One Easter Sunday morning I was waxing eloquent and said without thinking, "I'm sure we have all used our imaginations! I sure have. Why I've even been a king on my throne with all my concubines!" Ramona was sitting by the pastor's wife and later told me Jean Crandall was trying so hard to keep from laughing out loud she was shaking all over.

After one Sunday night service in South Dakota, a good number of people gathered in the large prayer room complete with a platform and a piano just off the sanctuary which they used for adult classes and some midweek services. I noticed a guy who had taken his shoes off which I thought was a bit odd, and then I was quite shocked when he sat down at the piano with his hands poised over the keyboard for what must have been a full minute and then shouted, "Now, in Jesus name!" and proceeded to try to play the piano with divine intervention. Let me tell you, there was nothing divine about any of it. After less than a minute, he quietly picked up his shoes and tiptoed out of the prayer room in his stocking feet, completely humbled. That was the last I ever saw of him.

In the spring of 1961, I received a call from A. M. Alber, the pastor of First Assembly of God in Des Moines, Iowa. He wanted to know if I would come that summer and hold a two-week, all-church revival with an emphasis on youth. I knew I was going to be in the area and few pastors liked to schedule revival meetings in the middle of the summer so I said, "Sure." You cannot believe how shocked I was when I strode up the steps of the church for the first service, all prayed up with my Bible and trumpet, only to discover about 40 kids ranging from first grade to junior high school age. I had never preached to kids that age in my life. Furthermore, it was going to be for two weeks. I quickly realized the only all-church part of it would be on Sundays when I preached to the whole church. I had to come up with a whole program for kids almost instantly. Ramona was a big help on the piano as we sang a bunch of kids' songs we learned way back in our Sunday School days. I had them sing "Only a Boy Named David" and proceeded to preach a message on David with all the calisthenics imaginable. Then I came up with the idea of a contest with prizes I did not have. It was absolutely wild. It is quite a confession to make, but I did not have the motivation to prepare a message during the day or even pray. However, God blessed the effort; and by the time we finished the two weeks, we were averaging about 80 kids and they watched whom they thought was an old man tell Bible stories like they had never seen or heard. I did pray and prepare for the Sunday services. When I told A. M. Alber after the meeting how upset I had been to learn his invitation for an all-church revival with an emphasis toward youth turned out to be a kids' meeting, he literally roared with laughter and said, "It was a million dollars' worth of experience for you." Let me tell you, I never "preached" another "kids' revival" ever again.

We did have an interesting experience in Independence, Missouri, one day when we visited the new Harry S. Truman Library and were privileged to meet him. He took the time to talk to us and a few other tourists in a small auditorium about his presidency and leading the country during the end of World War II. Near the end of his talk, a tourist raised his hand and asked Truman how he could have slept the nights after he had ordered the dropping of the atom bombs. The question really ticked Truman off. He said, "I never slept better in my life. I knew we were going to save thousands of lives." As I remember it, there were no more questions.

For some reason, I decided to study theology during most of my time on the evangelistic field. Of course, I took time most days to study, pray, and prepare for the evening services; but for at least two hours a day and often more, I studied the great works of theology. I nearly wore out Young's and Strong's three-volume sets. Finney's theology was so profound it took nearly six months to really understand most of it.

To be honest, I had decided to simply mention my intense desire to study theology and go on with my story, but I realized it was one of the most important factors in the success of my ministry. During my years in school, including bible school, I had listened to teachers and studied enough to pass tests with the goal of getting through the educational process. My only motivation through most of my years in school and college was fear of being humiliated and called stupid. I was perfectly happy with a C average. The last year and a half at Central Bible Institute, I strived for good grades because of the influence of Dr. Donald Johns as mentioned earlier. I did not understand that schools and universities do not give you an education but give you the tools to educate yourself. I cringe when I hear people say, "I finished my education at such and such a college." I truly admire people who did well in school and earned advanced degrees and would never trade my three years at CBI for anything, but I have watched ministers who have advanced degrees, even doctorates, who were obviously ineffective in ministry.

In my view, a school or university can only educate a person "to a degree." They cannot teach the motivation to learn beyond their formal education and, more importantly, learn how to apply knowledge in life to the point of wisdom. In no arena or profession is this principle more important than in gospel ministry. The Apostle

Paul sums it up powerfully for his "student" Timothy: "Do your best [KJV says 'study'] to present yourself to God as one approved, a workman who does not need to be ashamed and correctly handles the Word of truth" (2 Timothy 2:15 NIV).

The Lord knew that my course of study even in bible school did not begin to give me a solid theological foundation for a lifetime of ministry so thankfully He put in my heart a desire to correctly handle the Word of God. He knew I would be confronting every kind of doctrinal error, both in word and practice, in the future so He guided me in such a way that I could recognize error. I learned a very important principle. If you learn a truth or bible doctrine well, it will not be necessary to study false teachings because the knowledge of the genuine will immediately expose error. Many years ago, there was an outbreak of counterfeit money. The government provided a week-long seminar on the subject and invited bank presidents to attend. One of the presidents returned from the seminar and told his staff that he had never studied so hard in his life. He said, "The funny thing about it all was that we did not see a piece of counterfeit money until the last day. We spent the entire week studying the genuine to the point that when we were confronted with the counterfeit, we instinctively knew it was fake." Too many ministers have tried to build their ministries on shifting sands of contemporary thought and cultural relevance because they never learned to love, study, and appreciate foundational eternal truth. To them, theology consisted of dead or irrelevant ideas rather than dynamic relevant truth for all ages. In other words, the context of their preaching became the contemporary world rather than the eternal Word. I will always be grateful how God, through the Holy Spirit, started my education on the evangelistic field after I had finished my formal education.

To put it mildly, the three and a half years on the evangelistic field were beneficial and enjoyable. The money was pretty tight, but God met our needs. The low point of our income was $21 for the first week at a church in California followed by $23 for the second week. We were almost broke by the time we drove to the next meeting in Newton, Iowa, pastored by Hilton Griswold who had been the pianist for the famous Blackwood Brothers quartet. You can imagine how anxious we were to get at least $100 for our offering so when I got the check from the pastor, we kind of hurried to the evangelists' quarters to see what it was. When we opened the envelope, we found a check for $302. We were so excited we jumped up and down on the bed. In the year I wrote this account, it was the equivalent of $1,800. I will always be grateful for the years we were allowed to travel; have our needs met; meet wonderful people; and see many people saved, healed, and filled with the Spirit.

The final days of my evangelistic career were very interesting. The Lord had blessed us with great success, and I planned to continue our traveling ministry for three or four more years. We decided to start a family and settle down when our first child turned three or four years of age. Near the time of her birth, I bought a new Chrysler New Yorker, one of the largest and finest cars on the road, figuring we could travel quite comfortably with the baby for a number of years. I had approximately seven months of revival meetings lined up in some of the largest AG churches in the nation. We were all set, but God had other plans.

Near the time for the birth of our daughter, Ramona decided to go back to Pampa, Texas, to be with her parents while I continued to travel alone for three or four weeks. Her mother, Meda, was a nurse which was a real bonus and gave Ramona a great sense of well-being.

Two weeks before the due date, I joined Ramona to be there for the "big event."

As I was walking into First Assembly on the second Wednesday night in Pampa, I heard a woman say, "Wait a minute! I see him coming in for bible study. I'll get him for you." She caught my eye and beckoned for me to take the phone. My first thought, of course, was that in the few minutes after I had left Ramona, she was going into labor so when I picked up the phone, I was surprised to hear a man say, "Hi, I'm so glad I found you. My name is Marion DeHamer. I am the chairman of a search committee to find a new pastor for First Assembly in Des Moines, Iowa, where you held a children's revival a couple of years ago. Pastor Alber has resigned, and your name was brought up as a potential pastor." I later learned he was in Sunday worship, wrote the name "Crabtree" on a piece of paper, slipped it to his wife, and asked her if she knew who it was. She told him it was the name of the couple who had preached the kids' revival the year before. He did not know how to get hold of us so he called T. E. Gannon, the district superintendent of the Iowa District. Bro. Gannon told him that he did not know where we were but did know that Ramona's folks lived in Pampa, Texas, and attended First Assembly and it might be the right thing to give the church a call. That is the reason for the call. After conferring with Bro. DeHamer for a few minutes, I told him that I was not interested in assuming a pastorate at this moment (after all I had just bought the New Yorker for travel); but if they needed a preacher to fill in for the coming Sunday, I would be willing to fly over and preach for them. He indicated that the board would like to "pick my brain for possible candidates" if I could come in on Saturday early enough to meet with them and give them some recommendations because their knowledge of good potential candidates was very limited. I agreed to do that.

Can you believe that Wednesday night after the phone call and the bible study, Ramona went into labor and Renee Elizabeth Crabtree was born around 7 a.m. Thursday morning weighing in at a mighty 6 pounds 3 ounces. In those days the hospitals did not allow the fathers to be in the delivery room; but soon after she was born, I was able to hold her for the first time. I cannot describe the feeling of joy, the concern for Ramona, and the weight of responsibility. For me, it was one of the greatest moments of my life which, even now, is almost impossible to explain. At that time, they kept new mothers and babies in the hospital for a minimum of five nights if everything was normal. I had no insurance, but the total for the delivery and five days of room and board came to the astronomical sum of just under $200. (It turned out that Renee was worth every penny.)

It was clear that Ramona and the baby would be well taken care of at the hospital for almost a week so I boarded the plane early Saturday morning from Amarillo, Texas, to Des Moines, Iowa, to preach Sunday and help the board to collect some names for potential pastors. When I arrived, I was informed that three of the board members had gone to Ames, Iowa, to watch Iowa State take on an Illinois team. They hoped I would be willing to meet with them on Sunday afternoon to go over names. Of course, I did not care a bit.

The Sunday morning service turned out to be exceptional. Because I was not "trying out," I preached with great liberty one of my favorite sermons entitled "The Balanced Christian Life" (body, soul, and spirit) with good results around the altar. After the morning service and a good lunch, I was taken back to the hotel for a brief respite before the board meeting at 3:30 and the evening service. During that period of time alone, I was told in my spirit to "wake up" and know that the phone call from Des Moines to Pampa inviting me to preach, the big football game on Saturday, and the change in time for the board meeting were all divinely arranged. I was to tell the board I would be willing to be considered as their new pastor. I will confess I was not happy because I had worked out a great schedule in some great churches with a great new car and a great new baby daughter. I really wanted to travel for a couple more years, but I had learned that God Himself offered His wisdom and order of direction in unmistakable ways. His directive to take First Assembly was just as clear as His call to ministry. So I swallowed my pride and told the board that if they wanted to consider me as their pastor, I would accept it as the will of God. Surprisingly, they seemed happy. That evening I preached on the subject, "This Generation Shall Not Pass."

On the Wednesday night after my visit to Des Moines, I received word that I had gotten 97 percent of the vote and was the new pastor of First Assembly. Of course, the total number of people who voted is not that impressive (39), but everyone seemed to be excited even if the new pastor was taking his first church and living his first week as a 26-year-old. I was the fourth pastor in their 20-year history.

We determined to move to Des Moines within a month. It is amazing how quickly I lost the burden or perhaps the excitement of an old assignment, the evangelistic field, for a new challenge. However, I felt it was necessary to fulfill one more obligation: a week's revival at First Assembly in Wichita Falls, Texas. I remember being a bit amused when the pastor introduced me as the new pastor of a large inner-city church in midwest America. My first thought when I heard him say that was, "Who is the real evangelist here?" The "important church" to which he was referring ran about 120 in average and was a mile or two from the inner city. At the time, greater Des Moines boasted a population of a little over 200,000.

You cannot imagine the fevered activity and mixed emotions we went through during the three weeks after I returned from Wichita Falls to prepare for our move. I did spend a number of hours on the phone canceling seven months of scheduled revival meetings. In those days there were no computers so all long distance communication was by landline phones or "snail mail," the good old U. S. mail. It took me quite a while to contact all the pastors I was scheduled to be with for the coming year. I was a bit upset that none of them seemed overly disappointed I had to cancel. As a matter of fact, not one broke down in tears or threatened to sue me for breach of contract.

It would be very difficult to communicate the feelings we had on the day we loaded up our new New Yorker with a new baby and headed out of Pampa, Texas, for a brand-new life and ministry in Des Moines, Iowa. We got a new appreciation for the scripture "and He made all things new." We started married life living in a small, furnished church apartment and then traveled for three and a half years on the evangelistic field so we did not own one stick of furniture or an appliance of any kind. Fortunately, we had a friend named Shelby Ruff who owned a furniture store in Pampa. He had sung and played with Ramona and her dad for years on a daily gospel radio program and gave us permission to stop at a wholesale warehouse in Kansas that he had used for many years to buy what we needed to furnish the parsonage in Des Moines. (In those days, it was quite rare for a pastor to own a home but few parsonages had furnishings.)

In looking back on our shopping spree in Kansas, it is hard to believe what we were able to buy for $1,200: a washer and dryer, a full bedroom suite, a living room sofa and side chairs with tables and lamps, a kitchen table and chairs, and a dining room table with chairs.

Everything we bought was of excellent quality (early American style) which we kept for many years and which helped furnish two additional parsonages. The sales people really got into it and, I am sure, gave us several undeserved breaks. The only person who was not pleased about it was our 3-week-old who showed her disapproval by keeping her mother changing her diapers the whole time we were in the warehouse.

# CHAPTER 6

**Our first month as pastors of First Assembly in Des** Moines was memorable for several reasons. The parsonage was not ready for us. The board decided to have the interior painted and install new carpet. Besides that, our new furniture would not arrive for a couple of weeks so we stayed in a very small, very ordinary room in a very nondescript establishment called the Blue Bird Motel for almost three weeks. It was quite a challenge with a new baby; however, our first Sunday as pastors was wonderful. The church met us with welcome posters and a banner.

They even had a little corsage for Renee. My first sermon as the new pastor was entitled "I Will Build My Church," and that night I preached a sermon of faith entitled "The Revolution of Rising Expectations." There was a sense of God's presence and approval the whole day.

My weekly salary was computed by a rather unique formula which I had never heard of before or since. I was to receive half of the church's income from the Sunday's offerings up to $135. One time on a bad weather Sunday, the church took in less than $200 but the board decided to go ahead and give me the full $135 anyway. Soon after, someone on the board pointed out that if they were going to make up the difference for a bad Sunday, it was rather ridiculous to tie my weekly salary to half an arbitrary figure and set the salary at $135. They were pretty safe because the church was taking in an average of over $1,000 a week after our first month or two as pastors.

During my initial interview before I was elected as pastor, I was told the church had authorized the board to look for some acreage with a view to relocating because they were landlocked and had a very small parking lot in the back of the church. I naively thought that as the new chairman of the board, I would be expected to take on the assignment as part of my job description; and within a week after our move to Des Moines, I began looking for a building site. I was quite excited to inform the board during my first meeting as chairman that I had found a beautiful piece of land on Merle Hay Road and recommended we buy it. I wish I could describe the look on their faces when I told them. They had been "kind of looking" for over a year, and to have this young guy come up with a proposal just a few days after arriving on the scene was almost too much. To their credit, they authorized three of us, including the proposed builder who was in the church, to study the matter and bring a recommendation to a special-called board meeting.

Within a few days, the recommendation was ready; and at the annual business meeting in January, the church voted 100 percent to buy the property on Merle Hay Road where it is located to this day. The property was a little under three acres in size and cost a staggering $25,000. It did not seem to bother anyone that we purchased the property from a funeral home that had planned to expand.

Two weeks after settling down in our newly decorated parsonage, we were stunned by the assassination of President Kennedy. Only those who lived at that time can even begin to understand the shock and indescribable grief experienced by all of us. When Kennedy was elected, Ramona and I were holding special meetings in Canada. I believe that is the only presidential election in which I have not voted in close to 60 years. I would not have voted for him, but he was my president and his death removed all political designations. The main reason most evangelicals and Pentecostals had been opposed to his election as president was the fact he was Catholic and some thought his first loyalty might be to the Pope. Kennedy was invited to a meeting of leading evangelicals early in his campaign and succeeded in alleviating a lot of fears.

It is hard to explain personally; but when the president was assassinated, I felt like a close family friend had died. Every waking moment was centered on Jackie Kennedy and Lyndon Johnson. Things did not begin to return to normal until a day or two after the funeral. I believe every pastor in America, myself included, preached a message of comfort and evangelism the Sunday following the assassination. I later felt some of the same emotions after 9-11. I mention all of this to surface a sobering truth. The pain and sorrow of a national tragedy do not change many individuals spiritually over a long period of time. As a matter of fact, the churches I have pastored or observed after a tragedy only have a spike in attendance for no more than two weeks. Fundamental change does not come through deep emotions but through deep conviction. Emotions are wonderful and part of life, but they can be spiritually deceptive.

My first days as a pastor taught me how little I knew about pastoring in a practical sense. Even though I grew up in a pastor's home and completed three years in a bible college, the first few weeks of actual pastoring were traumatic because I was expected to be a veteran and not a novice. For instance, there is a big difference in attending weddings, funerals, water baptisms, baby dedications, communion services, church business meetings and other special religious functions and being the minister in charge. To the observer, the minister has a pretty easy job and knows how to do things by osmosis. Trust me, it takes a long time to become comfortable in fulfilling pastoral duties. The Lord did help me get through all the "firsts," but I will confess to a lot of bluffing. I learned early by following a wonderful directive. "When you do not know what to do—take over." For instance, I did not like the slipshod approach our ushers took toward their duties so I decided to "take over." I laid out an official ushers' chart with proposed head ushers, regular ushers, and substitutes. I wrote out basic rules and then held my first training session. I had never been an usher, but I acted like I was the world's authority. I informed them I would be watching them carefully for a month and then we would appoint a permanent staff and I would run the first ushers' drill. The new head usher would run subsequent drills. We did come up with a great staff, and I was never embarrassed with the way they conducted themselves.

As I have mentioned, First Assembly in Des Moines was running around 120 in average attendance when I assumed the pastorate in 1963. My paid "staff" was Bonnie Folden who worked four hours a week to help me with some correspondence and to turn out the weekly bulletin on a very basic mimeograph machine. We had some volunteers who kept the inside of the facilities clean. I did take it upon myself to mow the lawn.

One of the things that really bothered me about the old facilities was the placement of the restrooms. If you can believe it, they were located behind the platform. I prayed before every service that no one got the urge to go to the bathroom while I was preaching. Sadly, there were times when the Lord did not see fit to answer my prayers, and in the middle of the sermon some poor soul had to try to be invisible as they climbed the platform steps and slip through the door to the far right. Coming back down was worse than going. I think sometimes people just hid for the rest of the service instead of facing humiliation. The problem was there was no back door for them to exit.

One of the first weddings I performed was rather different from the norm. A few weeks into my pastorate, the governor's daughter began coming to the church. Not long after she began attending, she requested I officiate at her wedding. She wanted to keep it small and have it at the church. I was a bit naïve about such matters and told her I would be glad to help her. A few days later I received a call from the governor, Harold Hughes, who would later be elected senator. He was not a happy man. He told me in no uncertain terms he had arranged for the wedding to be held at the governor's mansion on Grand Avenue and wanted to limit attendance to the immediate family. If I had had a little time to think about it, I would have probably asked some questions; but I was really caught off guard and told the governor I would comply with his request. The wedding seemed to go off without a hitch, but I did notice there was very little happiness. To this day, I do not know the whole story. In those days, there was practically no premarital counseling which we now know is absolutely necessary. I never did see or hear from the governor's daughter or spouse after I performed their ceremony.

In summing up my first year as pastor, I would have to say it was almost 100 percent positive. I did have a few incidents that tested my leadership and lack of experience. A couple of weeks after assuming the pastorate, I was told that one of the pastors of an Assemblies of God church in a Des Moines suburb had been trying to entice some of our best people during the period of time between pastors at First Assembly to come to his church with the promise of giving them important positions. I had assumed he would stop as soon as I was elected but discovered he was continuing the practice. I invited him to meet me for lunch and proceeded to inform him I knew what he was doing. At first, he tried to laugh it off and said people must have misunderstood that he was just trying to have some fun and was joking about offering anyone a position in his church. When I began to name names and the positions he had offered, he finally said, "I can see why people would think I was serious and I won't do it anymore"; and he did not. We eventually formed a good relationship. I learned that the counsel of scripture to first go to a person one-on-one if you have something against them usually fixes the problem. If the pastor had continued to proselytize, I would have taken advantage of being part of the Assemblies of God denominational structure and brought him before the district officials to resolve the matter. If the minister would not have followed the directive of the district leaders, he would have been dismissed from the Assemblies of God. My father never did have that kind of biblical process available to him as the pastor of an independent (nondenominational) church.

Three months after assuming the pastorate in Des Moines, I ran into another problem with an Assemblies of God minister who had been attending First Assembly for a few months before I was elected. I found out later he had come to the church soon after the former pastor had announced his resignation, hoping to be considered for the pastorate. It came to my attention he had decided to start a new church in the Des Moines area. I suspected he was hoping to be able to pull a few folks from First Assembly to help him build a congregation so I took him to lunch. (I have spent a lot of money on lunches to talk through problems). I informed him that I had heard he was interested in starting a new church. It kind of startled him; and he said, "I've been praying about it and believe it is in the will of God." Then he said the words I had hoped he might say: "If I do, I have no intention of asking anyone from First Assembly to join me." I requested he let me know when he planned to begin his new church and we would try to help him. A month later he sent word he was ready to start his new church. I requested he come to First Assembly and let us pray for him. He gladly accepted. On a Sunday morning I had him come to the front and informed the congregation he was leaving us to start a new church in the Des Moines area and then told the congregation that he was a man of principle and had informed me he would not be contacting anyone from our congregation to join his church plant. We then prayed for him and sent him on his way. As far as I know, his church never got off the ground. In this situation, the Lord really did give me clear direction. You can be sure it would be impossible for any bible college or seminary to teach a person how to handle these unexpected and unique situations. I do know the Lord told His disciples that He was sending them out like sheep among wolves and that they were to be wise as a serpent and at the same time harmless as doves. I like to think of that as advanced spiritual psychology.

During my first year as pastor, I had to deal with a sister who wanted everyone to know she was a "real" Pentecostal and a "real" prayer warrior. She was the wife of a deacon, and her whole family was well-established and active in the church. I was as patient as I could be and let her outbursts go on for a period of time. I tried to deal with her as kindly and firmly as possible. After she had disturbed a prayer meeting by pounding a chair and talking in tongues with a very loud voice and disturbing others who were trying to pray, I informed her that she could not do that anymore at First Assembly because it was out of order and I had the responsibility as the pastor to see that everything was done decently and in order for the sake of the congregation. She turned on me feeling sure she was full of the Holy Spirit and said, "When Israel sinned, God sent them a Pharaoh and that is exactly what has happened to this church." Oh well! Surprisingly, she behaved much better and the whole family stayed in the church for many years.

The reason I have mentioned some of the situations I had to deal with early on as a "rookie pastor" was to illustrate that the Lord will give supernatural wisdom to anyone who recognizes their utter dependence on Him to meet the difficult challenges of life. That principle is magnified a hundredfold to those whom God has called to do His work. Anyone who thinks they can do the "work of the Lord" without "the Lord of the work" is only fooling themselves.

A minister once asked Billy Graham what he thought was the secret of having a successful ministry. The minister said Billy looked at him right in the eye and said one word with deep conviction: "humility." It does not take a person with a high IQ to figure out that the root cause behind the many failures among ministers is pride. The most vulnerable to this sin and ultimate failure is the "big" preacher or the most popular preacher because it is so easy to misconstrue the applause of people for the approval of God. They begin to think they are so special and deserve to have a lot of money and special "perks." They demand to be served rather than serve. When they sin, they do not seek to be forgiven with humility at the cross through the blood of the Lamb but to make excuses and be forgiven by their admirers. They have not learned that God resists pride and gives "special treatment" (grace) to the humble. Sadly, they will know how much God hates unrepentant pride when they meet Him at the final judgment.

One of the reasons many Pentecostals are not as effective as they should be is because they take great pride in being distinguished from other religious organizations by believing in and possessing spiritual gifts instead of being humbled by them. Even in secular society people do not like those who are proud and arrogant because they are talented or rich. I understand completely why many evangelicals resist proud, judgmental, "superspiritual" Pentecostals. I do not like them either because a few of them lived with us for weeks at a time in our home when I was growing up. At the best, all of their good works will be burnt up at the Judgment Seat of Christ.

The reason I have emphasized the matter of pride in the ministry is because I have seen the utter destruction of churches and ministries as a direct result of arrogance and selfishness which should have no place in true Pentecostalism. As God is my witness, I take absolutely no credit for my perceived success in the ministry. I will admit to a little bit of "sanctified greed." I do want lots of rewards when I get to heaven so I am reluctant to grab them now.

On November 3, 1964, almost exactly one year from the day I was elected pastor of First Assembly, we dedicated the new church building at 2725 Merle Hay Road. The church with all of its additions is still at the same address and, by the way, has the same phone number over 50 years later. A member of the congregation and member of the board, Dale Erickson, served as the contractor and completed the project for $150,000. The debt on the new church was $60,000.

Dedication day was thrilling. The new church was packed; and the district superintendent, T. E. Gannon, was the guest speaker. The church did nothing but grow from that day forward.

Probably the saddest situation we had to deal with in Des Moines was the long, debilitating illness of my mother. My father was so dependent on her not only for the home but also for the church. He was forced to resign the church in Bangor, Maine, in order to take care of her needs. For a time after he retired, he did his best to take care of Mother by himself, but it was not long before it was obvious her condition demanded constant care and expertise beyond his strength and ability. It was decided to move her into Valley View Village, a wonderful retirement complex located a few miles from our parsonage. It was an evangelical nonprofit company that offered beautiful apartment living and a highly regarded nursing home complex in the development. Soon after becoming the pastor of First Assembly, I was asked to serve on their board of directors. It was very difficult for my father to move from the northeast where he had lived and ministered all his life. I will always be grateful that my father put my mother's needs above his own. It was not long after they moved that Mother was confined to the infirmary in the nursing complex where she stayed until her death.

While my folks were with me in Des Moines after their retirement, I was not only deeply saddened by the continued decline in my mother's health but also the unhappiness of my father.

He had lost his church, he was losing his wife, and he was given very few opportunities to preach. I learned a very important lesson while observing his retirement years. While the ministry can be fulfilling and even exciting, it must not become the only interest or activity in life if it is taken away. I determined early on I would enjoy doing things outside my "professional life." While I still enjoy studying and preparing for the pulpit into my 80s, I can say with true conviction that if I were never invited to preach again, I would choose to accept that as the will of God and find fulfillment in my family, church, reading a variety of books, traveling, playing table games, cooking, and watching news and sports. I am sure that is easier said than done, but the only other option is to choose to be unhappy in the present because you can no longer live in the past.

A little over a year after moving to Des Moines, we were blessed by the birth of our second daughter, Rachel Jayne; and 20 months later, we welcomed our third and final addition to the family, Rhonda Lynn. To say life changes when you have children is one of the greatest understatements ever made. By far, the biggest change and challenge is realized by the mother. In my case, I went on with life and ministry pretty much the same as before my three daughters showed up. I was a terrible babysitter. I think they knew instinctively they were in the hands of an amateur. I remember the first time I tried it. Ramona went to some kind of a women's event at the church; but after an hour or so, I had to call her to come home because I could not calm Renee down. It did not help my reputation as a babysitter when Ramona changed Renee's diaper and discovered I had left a hair brush in the wrong place. It did not help to tell people it was just a baby brush and Renee should not have been that upset just because I was using it on the wrong end.

Poor Ramona tried to use me again when she was not feeling well late one night and one of the kids began to cry. She poked me in the ribs and asked me to see what was wrong. I did my best to wake up but proceeded to run into the wall like a drunk. I think I hurt myself. Ramona never again asked me to help with the girls during the night hours after I went to sleep.

The girls were a pure delight. From day one, they loved the church and never fussed about going to Sunday School. They formed fast friendships with kids their own ages. Every Saturday night before bedtime Ramona would bathe them and put up their hair in curlers. I never figured out how they could sleep with all that stuff stuck on their heads. Sunday mornings they looked like three little princesses. They were beautiful. On hot summer nights we would sometimes take them over to the giant fountain at the state capitol in their pj's. Winter presented a bit of a challenge. They would all want to go outside and play; but after ten minutes or less, they would be knocking at the door wanting to come in because they were so cold. Ten minutes later they were crying to go out again. After bundling them all up two or three times within an hour, Ramona would put her foot down and make them all stay in.

It was quite entertaining to watch them "play church" after Dick Eastman held a remarkable series of meetings at First Assembly. From the beginning, God saw fit to pour out His Spirit in great power. Every night for six weeks the church was packed, and many people came to Christ. At the end of every service, scores of people would be "slain in the Spirit." I will never forget what happened to a Presbyterian public school teacher upon hearing of the great revival going on at First Assembly. She decided to sneak in late after the service started so as not to be seen.

Before she could make her way into the auditorium, she was overcome by such an overwhelming sense of the presence of God she told us she sank to her knees and then lay prostrate on the lobby floor and stayed there for some time while God dealt with her about her need for a deeper walk with Him.

After six weeks, Dick Eastman held his one-week seminar called, "The University of the Word." It was wonderful. First Assembly was never quite the same after that revival. Many people joined the church; and most importantly, prayer became a more integral part of the church. Dick Eastman would go on to lead his great international ministry, "Every Home for Christ," based in Colorado Springs, Colorado.

One of the reasons I mention the Dick Eastman revival at this point is because the girls loved to play "Dick Eastman." One would be the preacher, the other would be the person wanting prayer, and the other would be the "catcher." Then they would trade off. At times one of the "audience" would be "slain in the Spirit"; and of course, they had to be quickly covered with a towel or blanket by the "catcher." Dick had a great laugh when we told him about it later. They also liked to play "wedding." One would be the bride, another the preacher, and the other the groom. It was not always a "Christian wedding" because often all three wanted to be the bride at the same time causing pretty strong fusses.

One of the main reasons for the growth and development of First Assembly was the highly successful and exciting missions conventions we developed. I learned first of all that the main speaker must not only have a passion for missions but also know how to relate to an American audience. Many pastors made the mistake of thinking that a successful missionary overseas must be an effective speaker to impact an American audience. During each missions convention, I learned to introduce new missionaries or those whom we had supported for some years by giving them a 20-minute window each night before the main speaker ministered. I kept them to the time limit by warning them that for every minute they went over the 20-minute limit, I would deduct $100 from their honorarium. I was nice about it, but they got the message that I was serious. No one ever went over. We started each service with one song and prayer. I would then introduce the first speaker followed by an offering for that speaker and then introduce the main speaker. We seldom went beyond 90 minutes.

One of the most effective missions spokesmen in the world at that time and would remain so for over 50 years was my brother-in-law, Bob Hoskins (who would later be the founder of One Hope that at the time of this writing has just given its 1.3 billionth Book of Hope Bible worldwide). He was our first main missions convention speaker and was used of God to enable First Assembly to soon become the leading missions giving church in the Iowa District and later in the top ten in the Assemblies of God. The quality of missions speakers we were blessed to have was impressive. We would do our best to secure them at least two years in advance. Other very effective missions speakers were Sam Johnson, Bernard Johnson, Wes Hurst, and Otis Keener, among others.

Another key to our convention was the annual missions banquet held Saturday night. What a time we had. We offered at least three different kinds of ethnic foods plus a standard American menu. Our people took great pride in cooking the food. The meal was followed by a short program of music and missions reports from the past year and then a brief message from our main speaker. I learned not to emphasize giving at the banquet but did have offering containers at each table for those who wished to help defray some of the expenses. I believe it is a mistake to press hard for money in every service during a convention.

The final Sunday of our missions conventions was always Faith Promise Sunday, and the results were always gratifying. Every year the giving grew, and we were able to take on more missionaries and projects. I found it wise to commit no more than half of the faith promise income to monthly support of individual missionaries for two reasons. The first was the possibility that some of the largest donors could move away or we could have a deep recession during the coming year; and the second was that large, exciting projects brought continued motivation and interest to the missions program. It is interesting to note that most of the time the actual giving exceeded the faith promises in any given year. It was also my experience that faith promise giving increased all kinds of giving including tithes. We had many testimonies of people who gave a faith promise beyond their means and experienced unquestioned miracles of divine provision the coming year. As one of my friends used to say, "If I became the pastor of a financially sick church, I would immediately put it on a missions diet."

Because First Assembly grew so dramatically in missions, I was one of the youngest, if not the youngest, pastor ever to be appointed to the World Missions Board of the Assemblies of God. I doubt seriously if I ever added much to the board, but I believe God used it to educate me on how to put together an efficient agenda and run an effective board meeting. More importantly, I gained a deep appreciation for the integrity of the Assemblies of God in protecting their doctrine worldwide and also making certain the needs of their missionaries were met. Every penny placed in their hands was recorded and dispensed where it was designated. It is not just my opinion but my deep conviction that the Assemblies of God has the most effective and trustworthy missions program of any denomination in the world today.

While serving on the World Missions Board, I became aware of many religious con artists who did not want to be aligned with any credible organization because they refused to be accountable to anyone but themselves, especially in financial matters. I had been raised in a home and an independent church that had shown me nothing but integrity and frugality in the area of finance. My father's church board consisted for the purpose of meeting the criteria of a nonprofit corporation so people could legally write off their tithes and offerings. When I was growing up, very few people in our church made enough money to pay taxes or kept records of their giving; but the few who did were deeply appreciative of the way my father handled "God's money." As mentioned before, he never took more than $100 a week for his salary.

As a member of the World Missions Board of the Assemblies of God, I soon learned there were a significant number of preachers who did not live and minister the way my father did. They formed a small board consisting of family members and close friends for the purpose of building personal fortunes through taking money under false pretenses or appealing to the emotions of vulnerable people who did not demand accountability. I heard reports and saw the results of surveys that made me very angry. It was not uncommon for the leaders of these "ministries" to pocket 80-90 percent of the money they took in from their fundraising with made up "sob stories" and emotional appeals for themselves. As a pastor, it was very difficult to warn my people of who they were and what they were doing for several reasons. There are some very effective and honest independent ministries that do a great work, but it is hard to know for sure unless you know them personally or are given access to their audited financial statements. Unscrupulous operators will often publish all kinds of false reports of miracles and sizes of crowds but hate accountability to their donors. They are "offended" when they are asked to provide verifiable financial statements.

On the other hand, people who are operating with integrity are more than pleased to open their books to potential donors. I learned the best way to protect my people in the area of missions giving was to "overcome evil with good" by teaching them to give through the local church to ministries approved and made accountable to their own denomination. Missions conventions gave my people the opportunity to hear directly from some of the greatest missionaries in the world and know that every penny they gave would go for the purpose it was given.

A few weeks after arriving in Des Moines, I was in prayer asking the Lord for wisdom in how to lead the church forward. I realized I was a complete novice at being a pastor in spite of the fact I had been raised in a pastor's home, graduated from a great bible college, and served and learned from pastors in my role as an intern and assistant. To add to my pastoral education, I had the privilege of working with and observing scores of pastors for over three years as an evangelist. I learned quickly that it is one of the easiest things in the world to criticize a leader until you are handed the reins and told that you are now responsible to lead a church. Overnight, I became a complete novice and felt ill-equipped to actually be more than a preacher but also a pastor—but not just any pastor but the pastor of First Assembly of God in Des Moines which, like any church, is unique in every way. No congregation like it, no board like it, no church building like it, no financial operation like it, no history like it, etc., etc. All I can say is that my prayer life accelerated. I do not want to over-spiritualize what happened, but God spoke clearly into my spirit and said, "Envision what you want First Assembly to look like in five years and begin to write a detailed annual plan, and I will help you." I knew instinctively it was a divine revelation for two reasons. I had never heard of such a thing, and I was thrilled with the concept.

I began the process of writing my first five-year plan by answering this question: "What do I want to see happen in every area of the church spiritually, numerically, financially, physically in facilities, musically, administratively, etc., etc., in the coming five years?" During my 25 years, I wrote five plans. The first one was only about 35 pages; the last one was 145 pages. I was planning to write the sixth one when I moved to Springfield.

My first five-year plan called for us to double in size with annual goals for every part of the church. That strategy did several things. An annual goal seemed very practical and doable; but for several years, I did not share the five-year goals with the board, only the annual goal. The reason is quite obvious. In a smaller church, a 20 percent growth goal was very aggressive but doable. They could visualize the church growing from 125 to 150 in a year but not to 300 in five years. If I had shared the five-year goal, they would have seen it as impossible and resisted much of my vision. The annual goals helped me to surface areas that needed special attention. They also helped me plan and begin training personnel to service new programs and greater numbers in every department. Each Monday morning while Sunday was fresh on my mind, I would sit and think about what area of the church needed more resources and personnel. In other words, I began pastoring "next year's church." I also began thinking of areas I could turn over to others. Through the Lord's enablement and blessing, I saw every five-year goal not only met but also exceeded. To put it all in perspective, someone wisely said, "If you do not know where you're going, any road will get you there; but if you do know where you're going, you only need one road to get you there."

In Des Moines, I grew more and more confident in sermon preparation. People often ask me how I preach without notes. It is almost embarrassing to admit that it is very easy. I use what I call my "chain of logic." I begin with three pieces of blank paper. On the first page, I very carefully state the obvious facts or objective truths almost everyone would say in their thinking: "What he is saying is pretty obvious." After I am done stating and clarifying the obvious on page one, I surprisingly move to the third page where I outline the spiritual lessons or truths the Lord has revealed to me in study and meditation. On page two I outline the process taking the audience from the known to the unknown with the goal of giving my listeners a clear choice in applying the truth to their own lives. On every major point in the outline I have an imaginary cynic saying, "Prove it!" or "What difference does that make?" or "So what?"

The secret of preaching without notes is to structure the message in such a way that in your own mind one point follows another so logically that nothing else would make sense. For instance, if I were teaching on the 23rd Psalm, I would begin my outline on page one stating at least three obvious reasons why David chose that analogy—such as David was an authority on shepherds and their duties. After outlining the obvious, I would move to page three and outline the eternal blessings, promises, and rewards of being one of the Lord's "sheep." On page two, I would outline the process of how the listener can make Jesus their personal shepherd in everyday living.

When I have my basic outline in place, I enrich it with illustrations and insights by commentaries on the psalm. I am then ready to write the message out in script form—not necessarily so I can preach it word for word; but in writing out the message, it becomes so clear in my own mind that I have no trouble in remembering the main truths. When pastoring, I would write out the Sunday morning sermon and outline in detail the Sunday night sermon and the Wednesday night teaching as well as the Sunday School lesson when I taught adult classes.

In saying that the "chain of logic" is simple to construct and follow, I do not want to send the message that the preacher can opt out of intense prayer and study to prepare and preach an effective sermon. I learned through trial and error how much time I needed to set aside to prepare my Sunday messages. On Mondays, I would determine what subject or portion of scripture I would be preaching the next Sunday. Then I would choose the commentaries and books I would use for reference material. In free time during the week, I would study any relevant material I might fit into the Sunday messages. I would keep my mind open while watching the news or reading current events that might be good illustrative material. On Friday morning I would head for a private place to study with my Bible and reference materials. I often "hid" in the public library. Years ago, I did not have to worry about the cell phone, but now I would put it on mute. The key is to have uninterrupted hours. I like what W. A. Criswell, the noted pastor of First Baptist Church in Dallas, would say in defense of his study time when asked about being unavailable in case of a crises. He would answer: "If it's that much of a crisis, it will be on television."

In looking back over almost 60 years of ministry, I attribute most of my success or effectiveness to the fact that early on I believed God had called me to preach and that meant preaching was paramount. I have never wavered from that conviction. As a minister, I had to do many other things; but I am convinced that after maintaining a personal relationship with Christ and faithfulness to my wife and family, everything else comes 3rd or 400th behind preaching. When any ordained preacher puts his preparation for the pulpit as the top priority in ministry, there are many wonderful unintended consequences. His messages help more people than if he spent 60 hours a week in personal counseling. He is more relevant to every age group than any specialist to any one segment of the population. He himself is enriched and blessed. The list goes on and on.

In a very few months after moving to our new location, it became obvious we would need to expand our facilities in a comparatively short period of time so we began to buy up houses around the church to prepare for growth and development. Just four years into moving to our new location, we broke ground for a new office and Sunday School complex attached to the back of the existing auditorium. It was one of the best things we ever did at First Assembly. It allowed us to expand the existing auditorium and provide new office space and, most importantly, more than double the classroom space.

Nearly every summer during our ministry in Des Moines, I was asked to preach district camp meetings. In those years, district camps were very successful and, in most cases, drew big crowds. I began my camp ministry at the Nebraska camp meeting which I would preach three times. The biggest camp was in Oregon which drew around 2,000. Instead of taking vacations, we took our girls to the camp meetings. It was a win-win. The girls loved it, met new friends, were enriched spiritually, and not only did our whole family have free housing and food, but I also got paid to do what I loved to do.

Just before writing my second five-year plan for First Assembly, I was asked to consider pastoring a very fine and comparatively large church in Wisconsin. To tell you the truth, I was quite flattered at age 31 to be asked to consider such a prestigious assignment. I got it in my head that maybe the Lord wanted me to write my second five-year plan for a different church. I mention this because what would be a promotion in the natural is often not the will of God. After visiting the church in Wisconsin and meeting with the board, both Ramona and I knew it was not the will of God for us to make a change in pastorates.

We returned to Des Moines where we saw the fulfillment of my second five-year plan in every area. As a matter of fact, the church grew to the same size as the church we considered in Wisconsin.

As mentioned before, I learned a number of vital lessons during my first pastorate. One lesson was both serious and humorous. For many years Kathryn Khulman was one of the most famous Pentecostal preachers in America. She consistently filled large auditoriums and wrote the book, *I Believe in Miracles*, which was filled with testimonies of astounding miracles throughout her ministry. However, I was really turned off by her flamboyancy and what I thought was dramatic showmanship. She dressed in long flowing gowns and came floating out on the stage to "How Great Thou Art." Furthermore, she owned a hotel; and even worse, she was a divorcee a couple of times so I decided God should not use her anymore. Her whole background and style of ministry was too confusing and raised too many questions among the laity.

Soon after making the momentous decision to ask God not to use Kathryn Khulman anymore, I went off to preach a camp meeting. When I returned home, I was informed by the local chapter of the Pentecostal Fellowship of North America in Des Moines that she was coming to Des Moines and I had been appointed to be the chairman of her "campaign." It became clear how much influence I had in telling God who He could and could not use. I was very uncomfortable with the whole situation, but I took some comfort in the fact that the "campaign" was one Sunday afternoon and that the role of the chairman consisted of staying with the guest behind the scenes. Her staff ran everything. I further reasoned that my refusal to be the chairman could do more harm than good so I found myself alone with her behind the platform curtain waiting for her dramatic entrance. For some strange reason, I went to her and asked this rather inappropriate question. "Sis. Khulman, why does God use you?" (I still cringe when I think of it). She must have seen my sincerity and took no offense. She threw up her hands and said, "I don't know. I've asked the Lord hundreds of times—no, thousands of times, and I still don't know!" I then said rather stupidly, "Well, thank you very much"; and then I saw why God used her. She began to pace saying, "God, I can't go out there unless you go with me." She seemed to become more and more desperate. She saw me watching her, pointed her finger at me, and said, "Pray!" with such authority that I did. I saw her grasping the curtain in desperation in prayer. Then I watched an amazing thing. She suddenly stopped, straightened her back, and said, "Now, I can go." I went to the side, gave the signal, and she walked out to the strains of "How Great Thou Art." I knew in that moment all the drama was not about her but about Him. God continued to use her for many years.

In 1965, the General Council came to Des Moines. For some strange reason, they asked me to lead a choir of approximately 60-70 voices from the local churches to sing the "Hallelujah Chorus" for one of the evening sessions. It went fairly well, but everyone stood including the people on the platform which made it impossible for me to see the whole choir at one time. It was very frustrating, but we made it.

I thought I had a hard time leading the "Hallelujah Chorus" until I heard my son-in-law tell me that the pastor where he was the music director had a sudden inspiration to have the whole congregation stand on the spur of the moment one Sunday morning and have him lead them in the "Hallelujah Chorus," unrehearsed, of course. I wish I could have been there to hear them try to sing the middle part. It did not go well.

In 1973, I was shocked to receive an invitation to be one of the main speakers at the General Council of the Assemblies of God to be held the first week of August in Miami Beach, Florida. You can be sure I was scared to death. I thought for a while I would need to take, at the least, a detailed outline to the pulpit. I was sure I would not only lose my "chain of logic" but my mind. However, the Lord helped me not only prepare a message but also to deliver it with great liberty with no notes. The context of the message was from Revelation 2 and 3, and the title was "I Will Build My Church." In the audience was a man named Paul Ferrin, the music director of Bethel Church in San Jose, California, who said to himself as he listened to me preach, "I could work for that man." It would not be too much longer, and he would.

One night in April of 1974 around 11 o'clock while reading in bed, I received a phone call from a man who identified himself as Phil Sondeno. (He did not realize there was a two-hour time difference between Iowa and California.) We would later have some fun with that. He said, "I am chairman of the pastoral search committee for Bethel Church in San Jose, California. Bernard Johnson has recommended you as a possible candidate for our church, and the committee has asked me to contact you to see if you would have any interest in allowing us to interview you."

Because of the success of First Assembly and my exposure at the General Council, I had been contacted by other churches and had been turning down offers to make a change. Furthermore, I was halfway through my third five-year plan for First Assembly and was pretty excited about the future in Des Moines; but a very strong voice in my spirit said, "Listen." The first thing I said to myself was "Uh, oh." Phil went on to explain that their present pastor had recently resigned. I asked Phil where San Jose was located in California. He must have been taken aback a bit because San Jose was bigger in population than San Francisco and located about 50 miles away. I knew nothing about Bethel Church but did know of one of the former pastors, Dr. Leland Keyes, whom years before had pastored the famous Glad Tidings Church in San Francisco and later served for some years as president of Bethany College. After talking to Phil a few minutes, I agreed to fly to San Jose and meet with the board. The meeting with the board was more than powerful. The Spirit of God settled over the room, and I felt I was already the pastor as did other members of the board. On May 9, I preached my first sermon at Bethel Church entitled "The Cedars of Lebanon," and a few days later we received a 97 percent vote.

The change from Des Moines to San Jose was not easy. We had to take some time to say goodbye to First Assembly. After ten plus years, I almost felt like a traitor leaving such wonderful people who had put up with my pastoral inexperience and had treated my family like one of their own. The board offered to double our salary if we would stay. I knew their hearts were right, but that offer clarified my decision to leave. Soon after saying farewell to us, they contacted my brother David who had pastored in St. John, New Brunswick, for 20 years; and in spite of the fact he had no Assemblies of God credentials (which he got quickly), he was elected to pastor First Assembly which he did for many years with distinction.

Before moving to San Jose, I had to preach a very important conference in Europe; so after my last Sunday in Des Moines, I sent the family to Colorado for a vacation and proceeded to fulfill my obligation in Spain. I then flew back to Colorado to help drive the family to our new ministry and home in San Jose. On July 14, 1974, I filled the pulpit at Bethel Church as the pastor. It would prove to be a wonderful fourteen-and-a-half-year love affair with a great church.

# CHAPTER 7

The years 1974 to 1988 proved to be very momentous for the Crabtree family and years of growth for Bethel Church. At the time I accepted the pastorate, Bethel was running an average of around 500-550 on any given Sunday morning. It was a church with a very interesting history.

In the early 1950s, a man named Ed Robeck felt the call of God to plant an Assemblies of God church in the city of San Jose, California. He literally planted the church from the ground up, using much of his own money to buy a lot and with pick and shovel began to dig the footings for the church by himself. It became very clear God was in the whole project. A couple of men who would later become leaders in Bethel heard about a pastor who was trying to build a building by himself and felt strongly they should give of their time and resources to help plant the new church. From the very beginning, God blessed Bethel Church; and in a comparatively short period of time, it grew to around 200. For some reason after three or four years, Pastor Robeck felt his work was finished and resigned. I am convinced there are some God calls to be church planters who are not comfortable leading an established church. Although I never met Pastor Robeck, I will always admire his willingness to accept the fact he was called to be a church planter and move on.

The pastor who followed Ed Robeck was a very strong, charismatic preacher and leader who attracted many new families to the church. Just a few years after he came, a new auditorium was built on the same property seating around a thousand people. Allow me to digress from my narrative and make a bit of a confession. I have been amused at how pastors answer the question: "How many can you seat in your church auditorium?" Only those who have individual chairs as opposed to pews can give you a definitive answer because the number of people who can sit in a church with pews is more of a guess than a fact. I have seen five adults look like they have filled a pew (it is amazing how much room a very corpulent person can take to be comfortable) while the same pew can be packed with ten adults and children. Unless I asked my ushers to take a head count, I found it very difficult to give a definitive answer as to just how many were in attendance in any given service.

The real fun I have had concerning the size of a church is when I asked the question, "About how many attend your church?" The answer is usually the combined estimate of every person including the babies in the nursery who attended on a record breaking Easter Sunday morning. When you ask a pastor the question, "How many members do you have?" you should probably ask, "How many active voting members do you have?" because they may give the total of members who are currently active, inactive, and even dead. In many Pentecostal churches, especially in the past, formal membership was not emphasized. I have preached in Assemblies of God churches who had a regular attendance of 500 or more and have less than 200 voting members.

Now I return to the history of Bethel. The growth of the church was nothing short of spectacular; but shortly after moving into the new sanctuary, it was discovered the pastor was guilty of a moral failure and was forced to resign. It was a dark chapter in the history of Bethel; but God intervened and called a great church father, Dr. Leland Keys, to become the new pastor.

Dr. Keys was perfect for Bethel Church. The church was suffering the loss of a popular pastor and needed a wise and experienced leader. Dr. Keys and his wife Annabelle (he was saved and called of God under her ministry) had long and distinguished careers in the Assemblies of God. After several successful pastorates, he became the district superintendent of the Northern California/Nevada District and was the president of Glad Tidings Bible Institute (later Bethany College) in San Francisco before accepting the call to Bethel.

Under Pastor Keys, the church was not only solidified but also grew in numbers. In my thinking, the church was strong for many reasons. It had several years of solid Bible and doctrinal teaching under Dr. Keys' leadership which would later prove to be critical in handling the Charismatic Movement. It had a music program second to none. The choir, "The Voices of Bethel," under the leadership of Paul Ferrin and later Laurie Berteig would become almost legendary. Bethel became a national leader in missions, both foreign and home. As far as I can find out, Bethel was the first Assemblies of God church to have a large and dynamic Single Adult program. It was also ahead of its time in ethnic diversity. Every year, Dr. Keys delighted in having the different cultures bring Christmas greetings in their languages. I had to laugh when they told me that old Bro. Longiotti was asked to bring greetings one year on behalf of Bethel's Italian members. He came to the front and said with great solemnity, "A Merry Christmas in Italiano," and sat down.

Because of advancing years, the Keys decided to resign in 1971. The pastor who followed them had a comparatively short tenure as pastor which was the result of a set of rather complex spiritual dynamics which were not the fault of any one person or persons. I believe the Lord had taught me some important lessons at First Assembly in Des Moines to prepare me to help guide Bethel Church past a difficult and divisive period in their history. I am convinced it was one of the main reasons I was called to pastor Bethel Church at that time.

When I accepted the pastorate, I soon discovered that the main problem that had caused division and unrest was not the refusal to accept contemporary music but the attempt to change the culture of the church from a traditional Assemblies of God church to a Charismatic church—meaning the desire to embrace new teaching or emphasis on the ministry of the Holy Spirit. Like contemporary music, there was nothing wrong with the teaching in itself because most of it was biblical; however, well-meaning leadership moved too quickly to embrace the new teaching and expected the congregation to embrace it and make it part of their lives.

The lesson I learned at First Assembly in Des Moines helped me to deal with the Charismatic movement within the context of an established Assemblies of God church. Midway through my pastorate in Des Moines, the Charismatic Movement became very popular. There is no question God was doing a "new thing" through introducing what had been the distinctive (speaking in tongues) in established Pentecostal churches in a wide range of denominations including Catholicism. A very popular book was entitled *Father Brown Smokes a Pipe and Speaks in Tongues*. It was an interesting time.

At the time of the Charismatic renewal, some pastors shut the door on it entirely and preached against it because many of their preachers and teachers taught different church doctrines and accepted a more liberal lifestyle including smoking, drinking alcohol, and other activities which raised many questions in our Assemblies of God constituency. After praying about how I should respond in order to help our people in First Assembly, I felt very strongly to use the opportunity to preach and teach a series of messages on a biblical Pentecost in light of the new Charismatic Movement. I determined to approach it the same way I had done in the past by honoring non-Pentecostal denominations and ministries but at the same time maintaining our Assemblies of God doctrine and lifestyle issues. It proved to be a very spiritually enriching time for our people. For instance, one time I asked a Catholic priest who had received the baptism of the Holy Spirit with the evidence of speaking with other tongues to come and minister to our congregation in a midweek service. It was quite a sight to see a Catholic priest not only praying for people to receive the gift of tongues in a Pentecostal church but also to watch him lay hands on the sick and pray for healing. As I remember it, God did affirm his ministry by healing a number of people. I do believe two or three spoke in tongues for the first time, but I am not absolutely certain. It was a remarkable service. That experience and others like it taught me that the God of the Assemblies was not limited to the Assemblies of God. At the same time, I did not have to abandon any of our doctrines or convictions to embrace new spiritual experiences.

One teaching that really helped our people to understand why God blessed so many different churches at different times all the while maintaining biblical integrity was a three-part series I developed. I must give credit to Dr. Wayne Kraiss for giving me the basic outline of the teaching. To boil it down to a few sentences, I dealt with the difference between biblical absolutes, denominational teachings, and personal convictions. Biblical absolutes are for everyone, everywhere, and for all time. There are very few of them. Denominational teachings are for the body of Christ in local congregations to perfect the saints for effective ministry at different times in different situations. Personal convictions are for one and should exceed denominational teachings. This was illustrated in my own life many years before when I witnessed the salvation of a gambler under my father's ministry over 70 years ago. Vince had been a heavy drinker and made a good deal of money as a champion checker player. He gambled with checkers instead of cards. He was very good at it. After a truly miraculous conversion at the altar, he said to my father, "I had something strange happen to me just now after I received Jesus as my Savior. A voice spoke to me inside and said clearly, 'Vince, when you go home tonight, I want you to ask your wife to burn all of your checkers and boards and never touch them again as long as you live.' What does that mean?" My father said, "Vince, that was the voice of your loving heavenly Father who knows you must give up gambling. He knows if you played checkers again, you would not be able to resist the temptation to go back to your old lifestyle. For you, playing checkers would be a sin; but listen to me carefully. I do not want to ever hear you tell anyone in this church it is a sin for them to play checkers." My dad was showing Vince how the Holy Spirit guides and directs the individual. In the same way, the Holy Spirit guides and directs the leaders of congregations to benefit the whole.

When I arrived in San Jose to assume the pastorate of Bethel Church, I told the board I did not want to make any changes for a year. I had determined simply to preach the Word and let the Holy Spirit guide us. I knew Bethel Church had been a very traditional church for many years; and in my thinking because of their recent past, they were not ready for changes of any kind. They agreed. To my amazement, within that first year, we probably made more changes than any other two years combined. A whole new constitution and bylaws was written and approved, we hired a new children's pastor and youth pastor after revamping both departments, and other minor changes were made. The lesson was clear. Changes can be made without difficulty if the board and congregation are shown they will not challenge doctrine or fundamentally change the culture of the church and if the timing is right.

My experience that first year at Bethel confirmed a conviction that had grown over the years.

An established church does not want to be led by new leadership from point "A" to point "C" but from point "A" to point "B." In other words, most congregations do not want a new church but a better church. They want leadership to honor who they are and what they have been as a starting point to grow and enrich "their church." If a new pastor does not want to recognize and appreciate those facts, it is better that they not assume leadership. Too many pastors have made the mistake that the moment they are elected, the church is now theirs to be what they want it to be and cannot understand why the congregation has the carnal idea the church still belongs to them. I have often said it is easier to start a new church than to try to change a traditional church too quickly.

I have been what I think is righteously angry when I heard of men who were not honest and upfront with pastoral search committees (the same holds true in reverse) because they were afraid if they disclosed their true feelings or convictions, they might not get the church. I have heard of men who gave the impression to pulpit committees they were "thoroughly Pentecostal" and then got up the Sunday after they were installed and told the congregation that tongues and interpretation of tongues would not be tolerated in the Sunday services "as long as I am pastor." Others have tried out wearing a suit and tie and then came to the first service as pastor in casual clothing.

144

If I were a congregant in that situation, I would have a hard time ever trusting my new pastor.

From my perspective, the years I served as the pastor of Bethel Church were some of the happiest and fulfilling years of my life. Of course, there were great challenges and disappointments as there are in any pastorate; but overall, it was a wonderful experience.

I do have to admit I was a bit humbled when one of my first official acts as pastor was to dedicate the cookbook published by our Women's Ministry. Like in Des Moines, I was a novice in that area but tried to act like I had dedicated cookbooks all through my ministry career. I will have to say I enjoyed some great meals from that "anointed" cookbook.

Another rather unusual and funny incident happened in the old building when one of our very proper ladies lost her balance and fell coming down from the balcony. Everyone knew she was not seriously hurt when her wig came off and rolled halfway across the lobby and she was able to scream at one of the ushers, "Get that thing!"

I was not only accepted by my congregation in San Jose but also warmly received by the ministers of the Northern California District. I was a bit disappointed when I was unable to attend my first district council in Santa Rosa after assuming the pastorate at Bethel because I had committed to preaching another district council a couple of years before that was held at the same time. Upon my return, I was shocked to hear that I had been elected to serve as the general presbyter for the Northern California/Nevada District. I would not be surprised if that was the only time in AG history that a pastor, having been a member in a district for only one year, was elected to such an important post while not even in attendance at the Council.

For those not acquainted with the Assemblies of God hierarchy, the General Council meets every two years and is comprised of every ordained and licensed minister in the denomination plus a lay delegate from every sovereign church. It is the ultimate ruling body. The General Presbytery meets once a year between each General Council and is comprised of three delegates from every district which are usually made up of the district superintendent, the district secretary, and one pastor at-large (the slot I filled for the Northern California District). In addition to the General Council that meets every two years and the General Presbytery that meets once a year, there is the Executive Presbytery consisting of the executive officers in addition to a representative from each of the eight regions of the country plus a representative for ethnicity, women, and a pastor under 40 years of age. The Executive Presbytery meets six times a year. The Executive Leadership Team consisting of the general superintendent, the assistant general superintendent, the general secretary, the general treasurer, the executive director of Assemblies of God World Missions, and the executive director of Assemblies of God U.S. Missions meets on a regular basis to run the day-to-day operations of the National Office and deals with a "mind-boggling" variety of issues and appeals from all parts of the Fellowship.

It was truly a great honor to be elected to the General Presbytery at the age of 37 because it gave me a lifelong appreciation for the unique personalities who lead the Movement and allowed me to make lifelong friendships I would not have otherwise had the opportunity to enjoy.

Furthermore, I learned to appreciate the motivation and reasoning behind good decision making for a large organization. The opportunity to serve as a general presbyter would serve me well when I was later chosen to serve in a national executive office. God really knows what He is doing when many times we do not.

Those who have never served on the General Presbytery do not realize how enriching and interesting the annual meetings are to the participants. Every morning before the conducting of business, we had a full-blown gospel service with congregational singing, prayer, and a strong message from God's Word. Several times, I remember the Spirit of God moved so powerfully that business was suspended for an entire session.

Much of the business in the General Presbytery became rather routine over the years. We listened to reports from the executives, department directors, and college presidents and approved financial reports and budgets. One of our most interesting duties was to approve what are called "position papers" which deal with everything from strengthening our position on fundamental doctrine to moral issues involving such things as divorce and remarriage, abortion, homosexuality, and a myriad of other issues facing the church. The position papers are not in the category of legislation but are produced to help our ministers to face difficult subjects with biblical truth.

In all the years I served on the General Presbytery, I can only recall one specially-called meeting and that was to deal with the tragedy of Jimmy Swaggart. The reason we were called together was to settle the dispute between the Louisiana District and the General Council. The district had ruled to make an exception and shorten his rehabilitation program from the normal two years required by General Council policy to three months. The General Presbytery ruled to uphold the two-year requirement; and sadly, Bro. Swaggart withdrew his request for rehabilitation. Some people strongly disagree with our stand on a two-year rehabilitation, but they do not understand that it is necessary for two reasons:  The first being that someone who has a moral failure needs a year to back away from ministry and concentrate on the healing of family relationships and a second year of closely supervised ministry to help them "make full proof of their ministry" in order to be effective. The second reason is that a moral failure by a minister in the Assemblies of God is taken very seriously and that younger ministers learn it is absolutely necessary to keep themselves pure because souls are at stake. I personally take issue with some Baptist denominations who do not provide any rehabilitation or a path to return to the pulpit, but I pray the Assemblies of God will always do everything possible to protect our churches. Our failure rate in our ministerial roster is under 1 percent, but every one is a reason for deep sorrow and soul-searching.

In the late 1970s, I became more and more concerned as a pastor in California by the growing anti-Christian culture created by godless higher education and politicians who did not seek the vote of evangelical Pentecostal Christians. On the other hand, I became quite alarmed by the apathy and even resistance of our church people to become involved in the political process to the point where a comparatively small percentage of our members were not even voting let alone showing interest in running for political office or making themselves available to serve on school boards.

There were many people (and still are) that believe religious leaders should not inject themselves into any form of politics. I firmly believe that any church should stay out of partisan or party politics but should stand up and vote for biblical morality and Christian values. I awakened to the fact that as a religious leader with moral influence, I must do everything possible to help stem the tide of immorality and evil rising in every part of the culture.

After much prayer, I decided to ask the pastors of our evangelical Pentecostal churches in San Jose to join forces and form a coalition to help our Christian community become more involved in the political process without getting caught up in partisan politics. Nearly every pastor was in favor of the idea if I would be willing to be the designated leader in the effort and thus the Coalition for

Christians in Government was formed. We made two very important decisions. First, we would provide a voters' guide for our churches prior to elections and simply list how each candidate stood on moral issues, being very careful not to recommend any candidate. Second, we would only take up one major moral issue a year to avoid being immersed in a hundred different appeals from as many well-meaning people and organizations. The program worked very well. One of the first issues we decided to protest was a ballot proposition that would, in effect, promote homosexuality in the local school system. We took out a full-page ad in the *San Jose Mercury News* simply outlining the many negative consequences if the proposition was passed. We then asked every member in our churches to get out and vote. In that rather liberal city even at that time, the measure was voted down by 75 percent of the voters.

It is more important than ever that religious leaders encourage their people not only to vote in every election but also to seriously consider running for office. However, pastors in this culture would be wise not to have anyone running for office speak from their pulpits. There were times I was asked to have someone running for office speak to our congregation, both Republican and Democrat, but had to turn down their requests—sometimes reluctantly and sometimes gladly.

By 1977, the growth of the church made it clear to everyone we would need to expand our facilities and, most critically, provide more parking. We were able to work out an agreement with City College two blocks away to use one of their parking lots on Sundays. The arrangement was good but not ideal, especially during the rainy season. Double services were considered for a time, but that would not solve the parking problem and the need for additional Sunday School classrooms. Consequently, the decision to create a master plan was made which first called for the dismantling of the original church auditorium and building of a multistory Christian Education and youth center. We would enlarge our parking lots by buying up houses and apartment buildings abutting our property. When we submitted the plan to the City Planning Commission, they came back with a very disappointing decision. In essence, they said we could not do anything to attract more people to Bethel Church. They told us we could reconfigure, redecorate, and do anything we wanted inside any existing buildings; but they would not issue any permits for additional building.

We appealed the decision to the City Council but were turned down 100 percent. It certainly made it easier for us to determine it was God's will to build a new church complex at a new location.

The board and building committee recommended to the church that we purchase a 4.5 acre commercial lot on Winchester Avenue a few blocks down from the famous Winchester Mystery House. (I would later tell people to go past the house of the devil to the house of God.) The size of the property was obviously not adequate for our needs, but one of our men owned a large office building on one side and a friend of his owned another office complex on the other side. They both signed an irrevocable agreement allowing us to use their parking lots on Sundays and evenings after 5 o'clock. In return, they could use our parking lots on weekdays. The arrangement added over 300 contiguous parking spaces to our property at no cost.

The building project moved ahead with very few setbacks. We hired a wonderful church architect named Dave Smith and hired Sondeno Construction Company as the contractor. It did not hurt that the owner, Phil Sondeno, was still a member of our official board. Of course, I stepped away from the building project itself and let the building committee with all of their subcommittees have full control. I only wanted to have my way on two issues.

I insisted we build the auditorium, education facilities, and offices first and Life Center which would include a gym, youth center, senior adult center, and banquet facilities complete with a commercial kitchen second. There were many families with teens who wanted to build Life Center first for obvious reasons, but I argued the church would grow much faster if we provided worship and educational space for every age group. I won that argument and the building on the auditorium began. The second thing I wanted was to rename Bethel Church to Winchester Cathedral. I thought (still do) that it would be a major PR coup and attract thousands of people to the church out of curiosity if for no other reason, but I decided it was not worth splitting the church over a name and gave in to the "traditionalists." To this day, it remains Bethel Church. I used to hear that some outsiders thought it was some kind of Jewish synagogue.

The plans for the new church called for a cross on the peak of the main building. A neighbor complained to the planning commission at the public hearing that at a certain time of the day, the shadow of the proposed cross would fill his back yard and he found the thought as very offensive. The commission agreed and ordered the removal of the cross from the plans.

The only controversy that arose in the building committee was whether to choose opera chairs or pews for seating in the auditorium. After much study and discussion, I was told the decision was made in a very close vote to go with pews. At the risk of sounding carnal, I could not have cared less. I knew I would be provided with very comfortable platform chairs because that was where pastors were supposed to sit in those days and I would be standing up preaching for most of the service.

The new church was quite magnificent: an auditorium seating over 2,000 (in pews), a beautiful chapel seating over 200 (in pews) with stained-glass windows, a grand lobby, spacious classrooms, nurseries, and offices. In addition, the facilities boasted three grand pianos and three new Allen organs—all for $5 million. I thought one of the most humorous exercises we had to go through before we were given a final use permit was to arrange for every toilet and urinal (around 30) to be flushed simultaneously to pass inspection.

Opening day was incredible. The choir, board, building committee, and pastoral staff all met at a designated place on Winchester Avenue. At a given signal, the Voices of Bethel, 150 strong, led the parade into the new sanctuary packed with excited people. We held a glorious two-hour worship service. I told the board we would have the dedication at a later date and invite a guest speaker, but I had decided to make an "executive decision" on my own and that decision was invite myself to be the speaker on opening day.

Not long after the dedication of our new church, San Jose prepared to host a Billy Graham Crusade. The crusade committee asked if they could use Bethel Church for the pre-crusade orientation. Of course, we were honored to do so. Billy Graham himself came to address the crowd who gathered. You can imagine how thrilled I was when he gave me an autographed Bible with a personal message. I count it among my most treasured possessions. In my opinion and in the opinion of countless others, he was one of the greatest preachers who ever lived. He has always been a remarkably humble man in spite of his incredible success. My brother David told me that Billy Graham spoke at a single service in St. John, New Brunswick, while he was pastoring there. When the chairman of the meeting introduced Billy Graham and the team, the audience stood and applauded. David said that as the team came from the side of the auditorium to the platform, Billy seemed to be uncertain as to why everyone was clapping and proceeded to start clapping also though he did not know it was for him. He was also a very wise man who avoided any situations which could have raised questions concerning his character. For instance, he would not go into his hotel room without first having one of his staff go with him to make certain no one was waiting to trap him.

Something many would call insignificant had a profound effect on me when Billy Graham spoke at Bethel. I was very careful to provide reserved seating for my entire staff because I wanted them to be sure they would never forget the experience and have the benefit of having some of the best seats in the house. After it was over, I said to one of my young staff members, "Wasn't Billy Graham great?" His answer almost shocked me. He said, "To tell you the truth, I've heard better. I thought he was a bit boring." Think of it! Bored in the presence of greatness! I knew then that unless that young man had a true change of heart, he would have problems in ministry. Sadly, my prediction turned out to be true.

Billy Graham died in 2018 at the age of 99. By a rare coincidence, I was unable to watch his funeral on live TV because I was in Colorado Springs, Colorado, preaching the funeral of Paul Ferrin, my former music pastor at Bethel Church and longtime special friend at the very same time.

Another great personality visited Bethel Church. At that time, Yongii Cho was the pastor of the largest church in the world in Seoul, Korea. The leadership of the Korean District Council of California invited him to be their guest speaker and was thrilled when he agreed to come. They contacted me and asked if I would let them use our facilities because they anticipated a large crowd. In checking our calendar, I decided the date of their council would not interfere with any of our church events and invited them to come. In the early afternoon prior to the beginning of the Korean Council, Pastor Cho came by to see the church and meet briefly with their committee. I met him at our reception desk and then invited him to the auditorium. When we walked in, he turned to me and said in his rather broken English, "This Pentecostal chuch?" I said, "Yes, Bro. Cho. It is a very Pentecostal church. We have many saved and filled with the Holy Spirit on a regular basis." He then asked, "You have tree tosand memba?" I said, "No, Bro. Cho, about two thousand come to church." He then said, "First Pentecostal church tree tosand memba first day." I did not tell him I knew he had started his first church in Seoul in a vacated garage.

Financially, Bethel Church was very strong in spite of building a $5 million facility. Prior to moving to Winchester, the church had a little over a million dollars in the building fund.

Before the new church was completed, we sold the old church facility on Moorpark for a million dollars to a fine evangelical church so our debt was comparatively small. Our congregation grew by several hundred in just a few months, and the giving reflected the added growth. We were able to add a number of new staff, and the programs of the church thrived. It was not long before we had to appoint another building committee and get ready to build a Life Center for the youth and other programs.

Anyone who is thinking about pastoring a church needs to know that everyone has an idea as to what they should do and how the church should operate. For instance, I had a multimillionaire member who was always telling me what I needed to do and how the church should spend money. Finally, I had had enough; and when he told me the choir needed to buy new robes, I told me if he would give the first $1,000, I would make it happen. This caught him by surprise; and he said, "I don't have that kind of money." He never again made another suggestion to me involving money.

It should come as no surprise that in many ways a large church is easier to pastor for the simple reason that a difference of opinion in a small church has a great influence and can be very disruptive, but it is rare that a single individual or family has the ability to cause division in a large church. For instance, in one week I was informed a family was leaving the church because we were "too Pentecostal"; and in the same week, I was told another family was leaving because our church was "not Pentecostal enough." In a small church that would be almost catastrophic; but in a larger church, most people did not even know what had happened. I hated to lose any people, but I did take some comfort that overall Bethel was a middle-of-the-road Pentecostal church. It proved to me again that a pastor has to be sensitive to people's opinions but must learn to make decisions based on principle and conviction, not fear.

Everyone seemed pleased with the new home and exciting ministries of Bethel Church, but I did get a rather interesting letter from an anonymous visitor. It had been my policy for some time to tell the secretarial staff not to pass on any anonymous correspondence to me because it did nothing but frustrate me and I had no interest in reading anything from anyone too cowardly to identify themselves. A few months after moving into the new church, the staff came to me and said, "We know you don't like anonymous letters, but you just have to read this one." The letter read something like this: "I recently visited your new church and thought I would give you some constructive criticism that might help you. When I drove in, I noticed that your landscaping needed some attention. Your trees and bushes are way too small for the size of your building (maybe because they were only about four months old?). I drove by your reserved parking spot which signals special privilege to the "average person," and I was a bit dismayed to see a new Lincoln

Continental which is way too ostentatious for a minister of the gospel." He did not know the Lincoln dealer was a good friend and attended the church and thought it was good advertisement for his company for me to drive a Lincoln. Consequently, he would offer me a new one at his cost and then throw in a contribution of $5,000 from his PR budget. I do not think I am the smartest person in the world, but I am not a complete idiot since he did not ask me to promote his business in any way. The letter continued. "When I walked in, I noticed that the grand piano was black and the organ was brown which was quite distracting. I also took note of the fact you wore winter colors and you should wear autumn or fall colors." When I read that, I almost broke into tears and resigned on the spot.

Another anonymous visitor affected me deeply in an almost miraculous way. I was standing in the lobby after a Sunday morning service greeting and chatting with folks as they left. I was talking to Phil Sondeno, our contractor, about Life Center; and I suddenly felt something pressed into my hand. I turned to see who it was and noticed a man leaving I did not recognize. When I opened my hand, I was amazed to see a beautiful watch. I said to Phil, "Look what that guy just gave me!" Phil said, "Let me see it." I handed it to him and he said, "Wow, that's a Rolex!" I then asked rather naïvely, "What's a Rolex?" (now who's the idiot?). He said, "Pastor, a Rolex is a very expensive watch. This looks like it is made with 14 carat gold." Of course, I was stunned and said to Phil, "There is no way I can accept such an expensive gift from someone I don't think I have ever seen before." Phil then said, "You'll probably hear from him pretty soon."

A few days later, I received a call from the man who identified himself as the man who had given me the watch and informed me he was putting the box for the watch and the guarantee in the mail. I said, "Sir, there is no way I can accept such an expensive gift from you." He then said, "I knew you would say that, but let me tell you the story and then I believe you will be pleased to wear it. Let me make clear, I am not one of those Charismatic kooks and do not consider myself superspiritual. I am a truck driver. I have wanted a gold Rolex for a long time and began saving up to buy one to wear on the weekends. Last week I was able to pick it up. Saturday, I began to put my new watch on and something said in my head as clear as a bell, 'That's not your watch.' I said, 'Well, whose is it?' The voice said, 'It belongs to Pastor Crabtree at Bethel Church.' I said, 'I don't even know him,' and the voice said, 'But I do.' Then I really got upset. I did not like what I was hearing. I had never been to Bethel Church, but I just could not put that watch on. I finally made up my mind to come to Bethel last Sunday; and I said to God, 'If this is really you, I want you to give me an unmistakable sign. This is crazy!' As you know, I came to the late service last Sunday; and God gave me that sign." I remember I had preached from the text, "He that ruleth his spirit [is better than] he that taketh a city" (Proverbs 16:21 KJV). I used the following illustration to help prove the point. I was a real fan of a great conductor named Arturo Toscanini. I had been privileged to attend one of his concerts when he was the visiting conductor for the Bangor Symphony Orchestra and I was an usher. He was a master, but he had a hard time keeping his temper under control. He had been known to have broken as many as a dozen batons during a rehearsal. On the twentieth-fifth anniversary of his being the conductor of the New York Philharmonic, the orchestra presented him with a gold watch. During rehearsal a few weeks later, he got so angry he tore his gold watch off and threw it on the floor in pure frustration. Then the man who had given me the Rolex said these words, "You then leaned over the pulpit and pointed right at me and said, 'If anyone ever gives me a gold watch, I promise I will never do that!'" After a long pause, I said, "Sir, I will wear that watch with pride." That happened decades ago, and I still wear it with what I say is "humble pride."

In 1983, I was honored to be asked to be one of the speakers at the annual Boston Sunday School Convention. It was a very large, historic evangelical event. I discovered later I was only the third Pentecostal ever asked to speak. That particular year, Ravi Zacharias, one of the great contemporary theologians, and three or four well-known Baptist authorities in Christian Education rounded out the speakers' slate. I found the whole convention a wonderful experience, but a "chance" conversation following the event had a lasting impact on the rest of my life and ministry.

The morning following the convention, I went to the airport to catch my flight, only to learn all flights were delayed because of a heavy fog (not unusual for Boston) so I bought the morning edition of *The Boston Globe* plus a cup of coffee and prepared to wait for my flight to be announced. In looking for a table, one of the speakers from the convention waved me over to join him. He was on the faculty of Dallas Theological Seminary and was also waiting for his delayed flight. After chatting for a few minutes and getting better acquainted, we began to discuss our differences in theology. I was surprised to learn his position on eternal security was not too much different from that of the Assemblies of God because he believed that man had a choice and God's foreknowledge determined a person's eternal destiny as a result of that choice. He was not like some radicals who believe man does not have a choice.

After discussing other subjects, he said, "I would like to talk with you about speaking in tongues." Of course, my being the ultimate expert on the subject, I readily agreed, hoping to convince him by my unsurpassed logic to turn him into a radical Pentecostal which God could use to make Dallas Theological Seminary a powerful Pentecostal center of higher education. The beginning of his discussion caught me by surprise. He said, "I believe speaking in tongues is a legitimate gift of the Holy Spirit as taught in scripture." Then he really did surprise me by saying, "I do want to be upfront with you and tell you I believe your strong position on tongues limits the ministry of the Holy Spirit in your churches." I thought to myself, "Look who's calling the kettle black." He seemed to read my thoughts and said, "I know what you are thinking. Let me explain. I believe you are so focused on teaching and defending the gift of tongues that you fail to emphasize the full-orbed ministry of the Holy Spirit. For instance, I believe the fruit of the Spirit is far more important than the gift of tongues because I have met some very mean and proud Pentecostals who think they are 'filled with the Spirit' because they once spoke in tongues." I suddenly realized that though I was not known as a mean Pentecostal, I was certainly a proud but insecure Pentecostal, meaning I was too insecure to emphasize that love, joy, peace, etc., were greater signs of being filled with the Spirit than speaking in tongues. I then heard them call for my flight because the fog had lifted; but more than a physical fog lifting so I could travel home, a spiritual fog lifted so I could better teach my congregation how to better continue their spiritual journey. Of course, I still taught speaking in tongues as the initial physical evidence of a supernatural experience of being filled with the Spirit, but it was not an end in itself but a gift to be used to become more Christlike and spiritually effective. I realized I had been guilty of teaching the gift of tongues in the same way as if I gave one of my daughters a brand new car who bragged about it as a gift of her father but never used it to go anywhere. My conversation with the professor did not change my doctrine, but it certainly changed my emphasis on the Spirit-filled life.

No history of Bethel Church would be complete without going into some detail about its music. When we assumed the pastorate, Paul Ferrin was the music director. He was probably the best and most well-known Assemblies of God music director at the time. He was one of the first full-time music directors in the history of our denomination. Before coming to Bethel, he had served at First Assembly in Memphis, Tennessee, for many years under a renown pastor, James Hamill.

Paul was not only a great worship leader and choir director but also well-known for his arranging ability. His wife, Marge, served alongside him as his organist. When the church was located on Moorpark Avenue, the Voices of Bethel put on annual productions of what were called the Singing Cross at Easter and the Singing Christmas Tree.

The Singing Christmas Tree became so popular with our congregation that after we moved into our new building, we decided to use it as a tool of evangelism and moved the event to the downtown Performing Arts Center which seated 2,800. We did not want to use our new church auditorium because it would have been imprac-tical and disruptive to our normal church schedule.

We built an incredible stage, supplemented our orchestra with some of the San Jose Symphony, and opened the first year at the Performing Arts Center free of charge. We soon learned that a freewill offering was not enough so in subsequent years we sold tickets. I shall never forget the collective gasp of that sophisticated audience when the curtain began to rise as the Voices of Bethel sang with full orchestra for the first time. After several years, the Singing Christmas Tree filled the Arts Center as many as 11 times during a 10-day period.

Our relationship with the San Jose Symphony grew to the point they wanted to be part of some of our programs at the church. One of the most successful was what was called "Evening with the Masters" which consisted of wonderful classical sacred music conducted by our music minister, Laurey Berteig. Ramona was, of course, our main church pianist; and with great pride I watched her perform with the Voices of Bethel and the symphony for years. She told me the night she had to play a Bach Concerto during one of the Evening with the Masters, she had never been so scared in her life. She played it flawlessly.

We had some miraculous things happen at Bethel Church through the years, almost too numerous to mention such as glorious salvations, infillings of the Spirit, and dramatic healings. I shall never forget teaching Bible study one Wednesday night; and in the middle of my teaching, I was "rudely" interrupted by the inward voice of the Holy Spirit saying, "Pray for Varee Bland; I want to heal her." You can imagine how frustrated I was and immediately decided I would pray for her at the end of the teaching; but the Holy Spirit kept saying, "I want you to have her come down to the front and pray for her now." Because I was about to lose my "chain of logic" and train of thought, I finally stopped and said, "This is very unusual to stop in the middle of our study, but I feel strongly that the Lord wants us to pray for Varee Bland right now so I'm going to ask Tom to help Varee to come to the front." We all watched as Tom helped Varee come down the aisle moving very slowly because of her advanced stage of Parkinson's disease. We prayed for her and then watched Tom take her back to her seat still shaking with the effects of the disease. You can imagine how difficult it was for me to continue the bible study. That night I beat up on myself pretty badly. It was a very humbling experience. The next morning about 7 o'clock, I received a phone call from Tom Bland asking if I was up yet. I thought to myself, "I am now." He said, "I thought you would want to know that right now Varee is fixing me breakfast for the first time in months. The Lord healed her while she was sleeping, and I think the Lord healed me too." I said, "What wonderful news, but what was wrong with you?" He said, "I have had a heart condition for quite some time, but I'm sure the Lord healed me last night and I'm calling the doctor to have it checked out." Both Tom and Varee lived in good health the remaining years of my pastorate and beyond.

Through the years at Bethel, we enjoyed a variety of great gospel singers including "Big John" Hall, Doug Oldom, John Peterson, Lillie Knalls, Dale Duesing, The Hawaiians, Regeneration, Sandy Patti, Bridge, The Palermos, The Cathedrals, Ann Criswell, Doug Lawrence, Johnny Hall, and others. Then one day I got a call from the agent for Vestal and Howard Goodman, known as "The Happy Goodmans." He informed me they were going to be on the west coast and would be interested in coming to Bethel on a Sunday and then use our facilities for three concerts Monday-Wednesday. I was not very interested in having them but knew many of our people would enjoy them so I asked him if they would come on a freewill offering basis.

There was a long pause, and their agent said we would need to sign a contract guaranteeing a minimum of $10,000 for the entire series which was, in his thinking, a very good deal because we would be able to sell tickets for the three concerts during the week. I told him to thank the Goodmans and that we would be happy to have them, but we had a policy not to sign contracts with any guests. I will confess I sighed with relief after we hung up. The next day I got a call from Vestal who told me she felt it was God's will for them to come and they would do so on a freewill offering basis. I agreed.

The Goodman revival began in a most unusual way. On the first Sunday morning I introduced the Happy Goodmans, and she proceeded to stand alone and began to sing a cappella, "Holy, Holy, Holy, Lord God Almighty! Early in the morning our song shall rise to Thee." I had been around great music all my life, but I confess

I had never heard anything more beautiful and anointed. Ramona said she cried all the way through the song. From that moment, we knew we were about to experience an unprecedented move of the Holy Spirit, and we did!

Vestal told me they had never experienced anything like what happened. The singing was wonderful, but it was a small part of the ministry that went on Sunday through Wednesday and then, at my request, through the next Sunday. Each service began with a short concert; then Vestal would begin to preach; and within a few minutes, she was moving among the people laying hands on some and giving a word of prophecy to others. I stood right by her, and she never missed. I knew most of the people and, in some cases, had counseled them privately. She spoke to the heart of their problem as if she had known them all their lives. It was remarkable. One of the most outstanding miracles I witnessed that week was when Vestal walked up to a girl in her late teens that neither Vestal nor I had ever seen and said, "Darlin', Jesus is going to heal you of cancer when I lay hands on you." When Vestal touched Michelle, the two girls standing on either side of her fell to the floor under the power of God. We learned later they were Baptist and had never been in anything like what they heard and experienced. Michelle was not only healed that night but later also became the wife of an AG pastor.

One of the most satisfying moments of my pastorate was the dedication of Life Center. As mentioned before, it had been part of the master plan for a number of years and I cannot describe the joy of seeing a long-term goal being met. I remember thinking, "Bethel is now a complete church in the sense that it has every facility for every program." For the youth there was a full gym and for the senior adults, a large, beautifully furnished room off the gym. The whole area could be opened up by pulling back accordion doors to provide a banquet hall seating 900 people, and the commercial kitchen rivaled any found in a successful restaurant. As a side note, I never did quite understand that the city code called for a sprinkler in the walk-in freezer. On the second floor above the senior citizens area and kitchen were two classrooms and The Crystal Room which could seat around 60 for elegant dinners and receptions. Of course, the centerpiece was a beautiful chandelier. Life Center was connected to the main church by an enclosed bridge over one of the driveways. On that bridge we built an impressive boardroom. One of our fine craftsmen, Rich Picone, took it upon himself to build the ultimate boardroom table seating around 16, comprised of different elegant woods. He built it on-site as one piece of furniture so the only way to remove it would be to tear out a wall or dismantle it. As of this writing, it is still in place.

During our years in San Jose, our three girls grew up and became beautiful young women. All got married and our first grandchild was born. It is hard to describe how thankful Ramona and I were to see them all center both their spiritual lives as well as their social lives in the church. The first year we moved to San Jose, we sent the girls to public schools and were dismayed to learn that Renee's homeroom teacher was known to brag about holding séances, and we noticed that Renee was beginning to be influenced by popular kids from ungodly homes. At that point, we made the decision to send all our girls to Christian schools. It was very costly but well worth it to know they were able get a good education in a wholesome environment. Some people think our decision was not wise in the fact that we protected our girls from the "real world," but we reasoned what people called the "real world" was actually the devil's world. At their young ages, we felt it would be wise to protect them as much as possible from godless influences until they were well-grounded spiritually, mature enough to discern between good and evil and true and false, and learn how to make wise decisions on their own. I am well aware of the fact that many Christian parents do not have Christian schools available to them or do not have the financial resources or be able to home school their children. In those cases, it is absolutely necessary to cover their children in continuous prayer, be very involved in parent-teacher associations, and make certain the children are heavily involved in a good church with strong Christian education and good youth programs.

Nearly everything we did, even at home before and after school, was regulated by the church schedule. Unlike my growing up years, our special guests at the church did not stay at our house (thank the Lord), but we had many of them over for dinner from time to time. The girls especially enjoyed the missionaries who regaled us with stories about foreign countries. It was a great education for them. We had several memorable guests including C. M. Ward, the famous speaker for Revivaltime, the Assemblies of God weekly broadcast on the ABC radio network for 25 years. Because I had known him all my life, we did not treat him like a special guest but more like a part of my family. He was a character. I remember his preaching at my dad's church in Bangor one week; and knowing it was a very conservative "holiness" church, he got one of his loudest "amens" when he said, "When you ladies get the fire of the Holy Ghost, you won't need all that paint and makeup. You folks in Maine know better than anyone else that when a barn is set on fire, the paint is the first thing to peel off." Two weeks later my brother David heard him at Central Assembly in Springfield say, "Some of you ladies would do good to honor God by coming to church with a little more paint and makeup. A little more jewelry wouldn't hurt."

C. M. Ward and Thomas F. Zimmerman, the general superintendent, were very strong personalities and often clashed. Bro. Zimmerman said to me one time, "Charles, if I could keep Ward on the radio and off the field, we'd be a lot better off." C. M. would often poke fun at Headquarters when he was preaching, and sometimes it did not set well with Bro. Zimmerman. One time the Board of Administration called him to task when he said something very humorous but hurtful to the leadership. When he was asked if he had said it, he claimed he did not remember it quite that way; but then Bro. Zimmerman put on the tape recorder and played back his words. C. M. then laughed and said, "Brethren, isn't it amazing what a man will say under the anointing?" Another time, when Headquarters had to raise the price of medical insurance, C. M. saw Bro. Zimmerman across the lobby at Headquarters and said in his powerful voice, "Tom, Tom Zimmerman, if you raise Blue Cross Blue Shield another 5 percent, the whole Assemblies of God will have to go back to divine healing."

C. M. Ward had one of the most brilliant minds I have ever known. His mental retention was truly incredible. I remember being stuck at an airport with him for over three hours waiting for a delayed flight, and he took the time to tell me the whole story of every first lady from Martha Washington to Pat Nixon including their maiden names, family background, how they met their husbands, their children, and their roles in the White House. My nephew, David B. Crabtree, called him one day to ask him if he could remember the source of a quote he had given on Revivaltime. He not only remembered the quote but also told David the author, the name of the book, and the edition he had read it in.

One of the treasures I kept for years were the notes I took from him one day when he so kindly gave me a three-hour lesson on sermon preparation at his home in Scotts Valley, California. He told me that when he had written his sermons for Revivaltime, he would sit at his typewriter after choosing a text and a title and begin writing as if he were preaching it. He told me he very seldom made a mistake the first time through; and if he did, he usually tore the whole thing up and started over with a whole new sermon.

His study was covered with plaques and keys to the cities where he had preached. I was more than impressed until his advance man told me one of his jobs was to contact the mayor or another leader of the city before C. M. arrived and request a plaque or appropriate gift.

In spite of his fame and success, C. M. was a delightful friend and not difficult to please. I remember one time Ramona did not know what to serve him for dinner so I called him, and he requested homemade pizza. When I took him out to a restaurant after he preached for me, he was very particular. One time we went to a well-known restaurant which I knew he would enjoy. When we walked in, we noticed an empty formal dining room with white tablecloths. Our receptionist proceeded to place us in the more casual area in a booth. C. M. said, "We prefer to sit in your dining room with the white tablecloths." She said, "I'm sorry that area is reserved for a large party later in the evening." C. M. said, "Come on, Charles, let's go find a restaurant where we can dine." So we did.

Another memorable guest with an incredible mind was Richard Dobbins, one of the first psychologists and ordained ministers in the history of the Assemblies of God. His clinic in Ohio is still in operation. When I told Ramona I had invited him and his staff for dinner, she decided to go all out with one of her very special meals. She also decided to make Grand Marnier soufflé, one of her most elegant desserts, to top off the dinner. I was a bit concerned when she told me she was not going to make individual soufflés but bake it in one large dish. At the end of the meal she brought in the soufflé to show everyone and said, "My husband said I couldn't do this, but doesn't it look great?" She proceeded to turn the soufflé onto a large serving dish; and when she did, the contents exploded all over the table. Dick Dobbins loved to tell the story wherever he went and how we all grabbed spoons and ate soufflé off the tablecloth.

In spite of the fact that each of our girls were very different in personalities, they were close in age and in friendship all through their lives. They were a great source of fun and laughter. We delighted in doing things together as a family. When I preached family camps across the nation each summer, we made sure the girls were with us and they loved it. They formed some wonderful relation-ships through the camps that lasted many years.

One year Ramona and I decided to take the girls to London, England, during their Christmas break; and what a time we had. I was not overly amused when they were so tired they slept through most of one day thereby dashing my plans. When they did wake up and prepared to go out to our first dinner, they proceeded to ruin all of their blow-dryers and curling irons because they did not realize the voltage in the bathrooms was different from home and needed adapters. In spite of the bad start, the experience turned out to be one of the great highlights in the Crabtree family.

During our visit to London, we attended some won-derful plays and shopped at Harrods, the world-famous department store which had several floors that covered a whole city block. I put my foot down when one of the girls suggested we buy a Rolls Royce which was on display. (One of the reasons I did was because the steering wheel was on the wrong side.) At one of the better restaurants one evening, the girls really charmed the waiters who could not do enough for them. When we left, they gave us a menu to take home all signed by the staff.

On Christmas Eve, we decided to go to midnight mass at St. Paul's. It is one of the greatest cathedrals in the world. We went early enough to get seats only a few rows from the front. The people around us were quite amused when one of the girls pointed to the kneeling prayer pads hanging down from the seats in front of us and said, "Look Dad, they have cushions for us to sit on." The people seated close by could be heard laughing. I was really surprised when one of the church wardens came to the microphone just before all of the pomp and circumstance began and said with his English brogue, pointing to a lady standing to the far side, "I say, this lady needs a ride to Devonshire after the service, and we were wondering if someone here could give her a lift?" A woman near the back stood, and the warden said, "Would the lady in the brown coat please make contact with the woman in the red coat, and thank you very much." I thought it was a delightful informal prelude to such a grand event.

After high school graduation, each of the girls chose different Christian colleges to attend. Renee, our oldest, went first to Central Bible College in Springfield, Missouri (where I attended), for a year and then to Evangel University (where Ramona attended) for a year. Renee was a great singer; but above all, she was and is an incredible people person. She was never a serious student, the statement which had been attached to me through some of my years in high school and college. "He never let his studies interfere with his education" somehow fit the maxim "Like father, like daughter" for Renee. After her shortened college career, she joined a wonderful traveling music group called The Spurlows for a couple of years and then met David Byerley, a brilliant musician in his own right who was like a son to the Happy Goodmans. They were married at Bethel Church and became music directors in an Assemblies of God church in Corpus Christi, Texas.

Rachel, our second daughter, attended Vanguard, an Assemblies of God university in Southern California for a couple of years when love interrupted her college career (which was a little better than Renee's) and married a young man named Bob Silva, a business major. To top it off, he was an excellent soccer player who grew up just a few miles from San Jose and attended Vanguard. They were married there in the college chapel. A year after they were married, Ramona and I waited and prayed for Rachel through 18 hours of labor. What a relief when our son-in-law Bob went running through the hospital shouting, "I've got my boy; I've got my boy!" That boy, our first grandchild, was Robert Charles Silva. Every week I would carry him to the platform and give the congregation an update on the most unique baby boy in the world. I would not be surprised if many people came to Bethel just to hear those updates.

Our youngest, Rhonda, attended Bethany College, an Assemblies of God college in Santa Cruz, California. She turned out to be our most serious student but once again love interrupted. A handsome young man named Gene Roncone who was a student at Bethany was encouraged to leave his church because there was no college or young adult program and try out Bethel. It is reported that when he walked in for the first time, he caused quite a stir among the female population including our three girls, but Rhonda decided almost immediately he was the one for her. To make a long romance short, they were married at Bethel and had 900 at the reception in Life Center. Rhonda later told us when they drove away to start their honeymoon, Gene turned to her and said with real concern, "Rhonda, it's still light; what are we going to do?" and she said rather coyly, "Oh, we'll think of something." And they did. Gene became an assistant pastor in an Assemblies of God church in a neighboring city, and Rhonda worked at a large tech firm in the area.

# CHAPTER 8

In spite of the very difficult time while my mother was ill, we had some memorable moments with Dad. We never let him forget the time he was outside staring at the clouds and made one of his most profound statements: "Well, it looks like it might rain; and then again it might not." He liked to cook and had the whole family over to his place for dinner from time to time.

Once in a while he would watch the girls for us at his place when we had to attend some kind of a special event. One time when we picked up the girls from dad's place, the older ones told us he came in from his room and saw them watching some terrible TV program like "Gunsmoke" or "Have Gun Will Travel." He said to the girls, "That program is too violent for you to watch." Rhonda, the youngest, about seven at the time, said with under-standing and compassion, "Oh, that's okay; you can go in the other room." So he did!

When my brother David took my place as the pastor of First Assembly when I moved to San Jose, he became their informal guardian—meaning when they had a problem, he was the first one they called. My brother called me one time obviously quite tickled. At the time my sister, Hazel Hoskins, was living in Lebanon with her family and working alongside her husband Bob, endeavoring to make an impact in that part of the world with their effective missions program. We were in close contact with them because the political situation was becoming more and more explosive and dangerous. Of course, my dad had little to do but to follow the bad news and worry about Hazel and the family. One morning around 6 o'clock, David received a call from Dad who was very upset and started the conversation without a greeting with the words, "Don't you care if your sister and the children could be killed over there in Beirut?" (he did not mention Bob). David was pretty quick and said, "Dad, it's 6 o'clock in the morning, I'm still in my shorts, and I don't even have a gun." My dad said, "Oh, go on with you," and hung up. Then David began to worry and got through to the apartment in Beruit. The maid answered and informed David that Mrs. Hoskins and the family were at the beach. David called Dad back and informed him he had gotten through to Hazel's apartment. My dad was instantly alert. "Yes! Yes! What did you find out?" David said, "The maid told me that Hazel and the family were at the beach." David said there was a long pause, and then he heard Dad mumble in disgust, "Well, they're having a better time than I am," and he hung up again.

A few months after moving to San Jose, Ramona came to the church on a Saturday morning where I was preparing for Sunday to tell me my mother had just died. We had watched her decline in health for over 10 years, a delightful vibrant woman full of life to become a bedridden "prisoner" weighing less than 90 pounds; and yet we still had hoped the Lord would raise her up as a testimony of God's healing power. The Bible teaches that heaven is real but death is still an enemy.

It had always been the wish of the family that our parents should be buried in Bangor because that was home to them in every sense of the word. A couple of days after mother's death, Ramona and I took the long, sad journey from California to Maine. The funeral director was kind enough to stay late and personally greet us. I will admit I was very upset and a bit frustrated with God. I remember reminding God of all the prayer that had gone up for her. People had had visions of her strong and well. I had believed for her healing right up to the time of her death. I have heard God speak to me with clarity just a few times in my life. People ask if He speaks with an audible voice; and I always say, "No, louder than that." He did that night while I stood alone at my mother's casket. He began with a bit of stern rebuke. "Don't you know that I am aware of every prayer that was made for your mother and I used your mother's sickness in ways you cannot understand." Then His voice softened, and I will never forget these words: "The other day I decided to answer every prayer in the affirmative, but I needed to decide whether to heal your mother temporarily or permanently. I decided she had had enough, and your mother is not only healed but also will never be sick again." There are times, even now, I miss her and wish she could enjoy some of the things we do as a family; but for her sake, I am glad she is enjoying heaven and I will see her soon enough.

In 1981, I lost my father. After my mother's death, he moved from Des Moines back to Bangor, Maine. There he had many opportunities to preach which he really loved to do. I remember asking him what he liked to do, and he said he "really loved to be in a good gospel service." When I asked him what else he enjoyed doing, he could not come up with an answer.

A year after he moved back to Bangor, he married a close family friend, Evelyn Allen, who had served as the official secretary of the church for many years. Every Saturday for as long as I can remember, Evelyn and my mother went shopping, had lunch, and brought home a bar of what they called "chocolate almond bark" for my dad. When my sister Charlotte was born, Evelyn became a second mother to her. Dad and Evelyn had a good five years together, and then his health began to fail.

The last time I saw him before his death was when he came to San Jose from Bangor to attend the dedication of Bethel Church. It was a long trip for him in his condition, but he "just had to come." I was deeply moved when I learned that when one of the family brought him to see the new church for the first time and he walked into that beautiful, spacious auditorium, he broke into tears. I can imagine the thoughts he must have had remembering what he had endured as a pioneer Pentecostal preacher—living at times in poverty, preaching on street corners and in tiny halls, and being misunderstood and ridiculed by much of the religious community and then to walk into this magnificent Pentecostal church knowing he would hear his older son David preach the dedicatory sermon in the church which his younger son Charles pastored. It must have been overwhelming.

A few months after his final visit to San Jose, he was hospitalized with kidney failure and would never go home. I decided to fly back to see him while he was still alive rather than attend his funeral. David was able to get there before I did; and when David told him I was on my way, he said, "I'm going to stay alive until Charles gets here," and he did. David told me my father's stay in the hospital was quite unusual. Many of his ministerial friends from the area and folks from his former church came to visit and pray with him. The hospital was worried he would not get enough rest, but David told them, "Look, these people are his family. Their visits and prayers will do more for him than any medicine you can give him." David was amused when Dad was served one of his final breakfasts and wanted some salt on his eggs but the nurse told him it would not be good for him. My brother told the nurse to give him anything he wanted. A little bit of salt was not going to make that much difference to a man who only had a few days to live.

I will be forever grateful I was able to spend a few days with Dad before he went to heaven. I was surprised at how well he looked. He did not seem to mind he was about to "finish the course" because he had certainly "kept the faith" right up to the end. I finally had to say goodbye and fly back to San Jose. I was home only a few days and heard my father had gone to heaven. The next day the chairman of our church board informed me they had met and felt it was as important for them as it would be for me to attend the funeral. Furthermore, they insisted the church pay for my flight and expenses. I will never forget their kindness and generosity.

When I got to Bangor, my dad was already "lying in state" at the funeral home. When I walked in and saw what he was wearing, I had to smile because it brought back an unusual memory. A couple of years before when he was still in fairly good health, he came to San Jose for Christmas. I asked him what he would like me to get him for a gift. He said, "You know, I like the looks of those new casual suits so many of you wear here in California. I could wear one during the summer back home." I knew immediately where I would buy him one because I thought I had seen an advertisement that they were running a sale on them at Eli Thomas, a well-known men's store. A win-win for me. When we walked in, the salesman asked, "Can I help you gentleman?" My dad said without a pause, "I need a good preaching suit!" They both headed for the suit department without even looking at me. I was in total shock. He was buried in the very expensive "pulpit suit" I bought him. I took great comfort in the fact he looked very handsome.

The funeral for Dad was quite an event. The church he had pastored nearly 30 years was packed to the doors.

Speaker after speaker gave tribute to a poor farm boy who had met Jesus in a tent and had simply obeyed God the rest of his life. To the very end he was a witness. Someone who had known the nursing staff at the hospital told about the last "sermon" he preached. It was late at night and a cleaning lady was working in my father's room when the nurse on duty came in to take his vital signs. They both thought he was in a coma and began to talk freely about the trouble the cleaning lady was having with her husband. She asked the nurse if she could recommend a good counselor. They were both surprised to hear a voice as clear as a bell saying, "Counselor, counselor! What's the matter with them? Why don't they go to Jesus. That's His name." Thus ended the earthly ministry of Clifford Alden Crabtree. He was 77 years old.

Ramona's mother, Meda, was a pure delight, a short little lady who loved the Lord and enjoyed life to the full. I will never forget her greeting when our family would visit. She would open the door wide and say, "Come into this house!" No one has ever made me feel more welcome. She and Elmo, Ramona's father, served as our senior citizens pastors for years at Bethel Church with no compensation and did a wonderful job.

Meda's family had a history of heart problems. Most of her siblings died at a comparatively young age, and sadly she inherited that weakness. At the age of 70, the doctor determined she needed surgery to stop the progression of the disease. She seemed to do well and was even able to go to Bethel a month after getting home from the hospital and see the new curtains she had worked so hard to have installed in the Senior Adult Center at Life Center. She was thrilled; but later that evening, I received word she had experienced heart failure at home and was close to death.

Ramona was a guest pianist for a special TV program at the Cathedral of Faith, a large independent church in San Jose. She had just finished playing a piano solo which "just happened" to be "When We All Get to Heaven." A few minutes after playing that solo, she saw two of our men from Bethel walk in; and she knew immediately they were bringing her bad news. Her mother had just died. Our whole family grieved over losing Meda, the lady with the tiny feet who loved pretty shoes. Her funeral service was attended by hundreds, a fitting tribute to a great little lady.

Some months after Meda died, Ramona's father Elmo strengthened the ties between the Crabtree and Hudgins families. He was attracted to my Aunt Gladys twice widowed. I warned him it was a bit dangerous to get involved with the Crabtree family since he had seen how Ramona had suffered, but I did not have much influence on him and he proceeded to marry her anyway. In my opinion they deserved each other because both of them were such characters. They had a good marriage in spite of the fact they were as different as day and night. They served as Senior Adult pastors for several years in the church Gene and Rhonda (my youngest daughter) Roncone pastored. They loved to pray together and listen to gospel music.

Aunt Gladys was always very special to me. When I was young, I loved going to her farm in Aroostook County, Maine, to play with my cousin, feed the animals, and later to pick potatoes. When I was about 15, her husband died suddenly. She later moved to California to be near her daughter, Marilyn Anderson. After Elmo and Gladys married, we had a lot of fun in the Crabtree family with our "identity crises." Gladys became my mother-in-law and my aunt became Ramona's mother-in-law. You talk about a "mixed-up" family. We had a lot of good times together

In early 1988, God began a process which I like to refer to as a divine conspiracy to make me willing to move to the Assemblies of God headquarters in Springfield,

Missouri. It began one Sunday morning on the way to church when Ramona suddenly experienced a terrible spasm in her arm. I immediately made a detour to a local hospital where she was given pain medicine.

Later she went back for a complete physical, and the doctor determined the cause of the spasm was probably psychosomatic. The problem persisted, and finally a new doctor took her symptoms seriously and discovered a tumor growing in the back of her neck in the cervical spine. It was clear she faced a very serious operation. The doctor told her she could be partially paralyzed or lose the use of her right hand and arm. She was playing the piano during the prelude to a Sunday morning service, and a well-meaning brother came up to her while she was playing. He stood there for a few minutes and then determined she was not about to stop and talk to him so he slapped a book down and walked away. She later picked it up and was a bit amused to see it was entitled *How to Kick the Devil Out of Your Life*. He had whispered in her ear, "Read this and you will be healed." She went up for prayer the Sunday night before surgery on Tuesday, but the Lord did not seem to see fit to heal her miraculously. However, God gave her nothing short of a supernatural peace to the point that when she checked into the hospital for surgery and was told they had lost the blood she had given days before, she told them to go ahead. It was a pretty grim group of people who gathered to wait and pray with me at Kaiser Hospital in Daily City before and during the seven and one-half hour surgery. Ramona reported that when she began to come out from under the anesthetic, she heard the voice of the doctor or God say, "Ramona, play the piano"; and she remembers being able to wiggle her fingers and knew immediately the surgery was a success.

A few weeks later she was able to attend the staff retreat we were having at a hotel in Sacramento. She reports that going alone to her room in the elevator, for some reason she said out loud, "I could leave now." Later she forgot to tell me that Glen Cole, the pastor of the great Capital Christian Center in Sacramento and an executive presbyter of the Assemblies of God as well as a close personal friend, wanted me to call him back when I was free.

You will have to pardon me if I divert from our narrative for a moment. During 1988, the Assemblies of God leadership unveiled what they believed was a vision for the 1990s called the Decade of Harvest with very ambitious goals which included a call to enlist a million prayer warriors to believe God for 5 million conversions, plant 5 thousand new churches, and train 20,000 new credentialed ministers during the decade of the 90s. I had heard about it but had not paid much attention to it. Now, back to the story.

When I did learn that Glen Cole wanted to talk to me, I called him back. He asked me if I had heard about the Decade of Harvest. I told him I had heard about it but did not know much about it. He then said, "Charles, we are looking for someone to lead this program, and I believe you are the man." I was rather stunned and asked, "Would that person have to move to Springfield?" He said, "Yes, they would." I then said, "Glen, I would have absolutely no interest in moving to Springfield." He said, "Would you pray about it?" I said, "No, I don't think so," and we left it at that. A few weeks later, he called me again and said, "Charles, I really feel you are to be the national director for the Decade of Harvest and I am going to recommend you for the position at the next Executive Presbytery meeting." To tell you the truth, I was a bit exasperated and said to him, "Glen, in just three weeks I am going to go to Europe for a couple weeks of ministry, and I do not want to be considered for the position." He said, "Great, that will give you time to pray about it," to which I replied rather firmly, "I wouldn't count on it if I were you."

Soon after Ramona and I with one of our deacons and his wife, Wil and Fon Balch, landed in Europe, something very unusual happened. For five straight mornings at 3 o'clock on the dot, I was awakened by the Holy Spirit and given idea after idea for the Decade of Harvest. After the fifth morning, I finally told Ramona about it and said, "If I'm going to get any sleep and be worth anything, we're going to have to be willing to move to Springfield." Wil later told me that he and Fon were worried we were having trouble between us because we were so sober and quiet during the trip. Of course, we did not tell them about what we were going through.

We returned from our trip to Europe on a Friday and used Saturday to try to reset our internal time clocks in order to minister on Sunday. On Monday, I spent all day at the church office catching up on details and situations that had surfaced during our trip to Europe. Tuesday was my day off; and at that time, I was enjoying learning to cook. I remember it as though it were yesterday. I was in the middle of cooking lamb shanks in honey sauce when Ramona answered the phone and informed me the general superintendent of the Assemblies of God, G. Raymond Carlson, wanted to talk to me. When I answered the phone, he said, "Congratulations Charles, you have just been appointed as the National Director of the Decade of Harvest by a unanimous vote of the Executive Presbytery. After a minute of shock, I said, "Bro. Carlson, I could not possibly accept your appointment until I have a chance to sit down with you and talk it through." He said, "I know that. The Executive Presbytery will be in session until Thursday. Could you get over here tomorrow and meet with them?"

The meeting with the Executive Presbytery was most unusual. Very little business was conducted, but the presence and power of God were evident. There was a message in tongues and a powerful interpretation confirming the vision. I knew I would be back in a few weeks as the National Director of the Decade of Harvest of which I knew very little about. I also began to think how I would tell my staff, board, and congregation who had been so good to Ramona and me for almost 15 years; and most of all, I dreaded having to say goodbye to Robert Charles, my six-month-old grandson.

Our resignation and farewell from Bethel Church was very difficult. I did take comfort in the fact that I did not want or seek a position at Headquarters but knew if I did not accept it, I would be out of the will of God. I had learned many years ago if the will of God rubbed the cat the wrong way, He would eventually turn the cat around.

Our farewell reception at Bethel was more than memorable. It lasted from 6 p.m. to after 10 p.m. It was tough to say goodbye to so many people we had loved and ministered to throughout the years. We had decided to drive some distance on our journey to Springfield but only made it about 30 miles and decided we were too exhausted to continue. Meanwhile, two of our sons-in-law, Bob Silva and Gene Roncone, had outbid three moving companies and were on their way with two fully loaded rental trucks so we could move in to our new home in Springfield. They drove day and night and would arrive in Springfield ahead of us. Our lives and ministries in San Jose were over, and we were ready to start a new chapter.

# CHAPTER 9

The first Sunday in our new home in Springfield we awakened to a snowstorm. You might think that was not a very important detail, but I will never forget it. For the first time in over 25 years I did not care what the weather was like on a Sunday morning. As a pastor, I knew the minute we had a storm prior to church, the crowds and offerings would be way down. This particular bad weather day gave me a sensation of great freedom and relief. It was also a sign everything in my life would be different from that moment on.

On my first official day as the director of the Decade of Harvest, I intentionally arrived at Headquarters a little late in order to slip into the back of the auditorium for chapel which, in those days, was held every Monday morning for 30 minutes. It was a strange sensation to be an observer instead of a participant. After chapel, I was introduced to a man named Charles Denton who, for all intents and purposes, ran the day-to-day operations of Headquarters. He could not have done more to make me feel welcome and at home. He had carved out a whole day from his schedule to give me a personal orientation which included helping me settle into my new office on the third floor; introduce me to my executive secretary, Sue Montgomery; have lunch with the executive officers; and meet key personnel throughout Headquarters and the Gospel Publishing House. I came away from that first day having great respect for the quality of people who worked there and how dependent I would be upon them to help me be as effective as possible in directing a national program.

It was 1989, a year filled with preparation for the actual beginning of the Decade of Harvest. Our team at the office worked hard to prepare materials for churches to use to get off to a good start toward reaching our goals. I wrote a handbook to serve as a practical guide with a monthly check list individual churches could follow with sermon outlines to help pastors strengthen the goals. I traveled to North Central University to make a two-hour video series covering the purpose and mission of the program. I was asked to preach the General Council to challenge the constituency for the coming decade.

There were many wonderful things I will never forget about the Decade of Harvest. Ramona and I had the privilege of ministry in nearly every district in the Assemblies of God. I remember one time we were gone from home for six weeks. Many districts and churches got on board and were truly excited about the goals that were set. It was satisfying to hear from our World Missions department who reported that many foreign national churches had picked up the program and were experiencing great results from their implementation.

For reasons unknown, it was God's will for me to serve as the director of the Decade of Harvest for less than five years including 1989, the year of preparation. The 1993 General Council held in Minneapolis would change our lives and ministries dramatically. We went to the council knowing that G. Raymond Carlson, the general superintendent, had decided to retire. I had very mixed emotions about a change of leadership because Bro. Carlson had given me total support and believed very strongly in the Decade of Harvest program.

Ramona and I sat in the back of the auditorium as the voting began. We expected Everett Stenhouse, the assistant superintendent at the time, to be elected to take Bro. Carlson's position on the nominating ballot. To our surprise, that did not happen; and Thomas Trask, our general treasurer and a good friend, was elected in subsequent voting. There was no question Bro. Stenhouse would be put back as assistant, if not on the nominating ballot then certainly on the first electoral ballot. Historically, very few executives are reelected on the nominating ballot because a lot of people like to put their own names in nomination or a friend's name referred to as a courtesy vote. As expected, there was no election on the nominating ballot for the assistant superintendent, so I prepared as with most others to elect Bro. Stenhouse. To the surprise of everyone, he stood and asked his name be removed from consideration in subsequent balloting. I turned to Ramona and said, "It looks like they will put in Bob Schmidgall" (an executive presbyter and the pastor of a large church in Illinois). To our amazement, he proceeded to withdraw his name from consideration. I then said, "It looks like they'll vote in Glen (Cole)," but that was not to be; and two ballots later Bro. Carlson announced that "Charles Crabtree, having received the required number of votes, is therefore declared the assistant general superintendent." Ramona and I sat stunned. Bro. Carlson did not see us because we were so far from the front and asked if I was in the audience. Then after a pause, he began to move on to the next order of business because he did not know I was present. Then someone near us yelled rather unceremoniously, "He's over here!" and Ramona and I proceeded to make our way to the platform. The rest of the day was a flurry of activity. Pictures, interviews, and congratulations. I was the most surprised person on earth. After all, I was the first person in the history of the Assemblies of God, to my knowledge, ever to be elected to an executive office without having served as a district official, executive presbyter, or executive officer. Before the evening service, the first official photograph of the new Board of Administration was taken. General Superintendent Thomas E. Trask, Assistant General Superintendent Charles T. Crabtree, General Secretary George O. Wood who at the time served as the assistant district superintendent of the Southern California District, and General Treasurer James K. Bridges who at the time served as the district superintendent of the North Texas District. We would become the longest serving Board of Administration in Assemblies of God history without a personnel change for the next 14 years.

At the election, I had expressed a desire to remain the director of the Decade of Harvest because I knew the office of assistant general superintendent was "without portfolio," meaning my duties would be assigned by the general superintendent and/or the Board of Administration. Bro. Trask felt strongly it would be best to appoint a new director for the remainder of the Decade of Harvest; and a very fine man, Efraim Espinoza, was chosen to fill the position. Looking back, it was a very wise decision because it would have interfered with my assignments and travel schedule.

In making a fair assessment of the Decade of Harvest, I believe history will record that the final results of the program were mixed. There is no question that the goals of the program were admirable and well-intentioned. I believe there were many souls saved and new churches opened as a direct result of the emphasis, and for that I will be eternally grateful; but as a person used to setting and reaching goals, I was disappointed in the final results. I do not doubt for a moment I was divinely called to lead the effort and would have been out of the will of God if I had refused to accept the appointment and feel honored to have been asked to lead the effort for a period of time. I do know I would not have been elected the assistant general superintendent if I had not served as director of the Decade of Harvest which had given me national exposure.

It is not in my nature to second guess any well-intentioned effort or doubt its validity, but I do seek to gain insight and learn lessons that might prove to be valuable not only to myself but also to others if I am asked.

The most important lesson I learned was that goals cannot be imposed on others. They can certainly be presented and they can be motivational; but in the end if a goal is not adopted and accepted as personal, it will simply be someone else's responsibility. In the case of the Decade of Harvest, many churches and even districts did not choose to adopt the goals as their own. I learned in a very practical way the difference between a fellowship of churches and a denomination. In reality, every sovereign Assemblies of God church is independent, meaning they have their own constitution and bylaws, choose their own pastors, and are legally classified as separate nonprofit corporations for tax purposes. The only authority the national church has over a sovereign church is holding their pastors accountable doctrinally and morally.

A home missions church is legally owned and operated by the district in which it presides. In most cases the district gives the church a great deal of freedom but is ultimately responsible for appointing a pastor, providing and maintaining church facilities, and approving budgets. In a real sense, it is more like being a part of a denomination than a fellowship.

In light of those facts, I would have used 1989, the year of preparation, to request every district to contact their churches and request each church to prayerfully embrace the vision of the Decade of Harvest and set numerical goals not only to be part of the national effort but also to use the program to bless their own churches. I would also ask the districts to help home missions churches set their own goals and determine how they could be involved in the mission and advance their status from a home missions church to a sovereign assembly. I would have taken all the cumulative goals to determine the national goals. My experience with the Decade of Harvest made me keenly aware of how dependent the national church really is, in a practical way, on the local church. The reverse is also true, meaning the local church must have a healthy respect and appreciation for their national office and leaders in order to take advantage of all it offers to enrich the local Assembly.

At the risk of belaboring the point, I believe the Assemblies of God had become more a fellowship of independent churches than at any time in its history. When I became a licensed minister in 1959, my perception of national and district leadership was one of great authority and dependence. That view was very widespread among my peers resulting in great respect for tradition to the point there was an unhealthy fear by some at times to be creative and innovative in operating our churches. Most of those fears were a bit unfounded because in time I learned that leadership encouraged innovation within the parameters of biblical doctrine and ethics.

By the time I was elected to office, the Assemblies of God, like all church bodies, had been doing their best to remain true to their mission and character and at the same time be responsive and relevant to the needs of the constituency. It remains a real challenge on every level, especially in the national office.

In my opinion, there are three major factors that contributed to the need for constant and rapid changes. The first was worship styles and contemporary music. I have already dealt with this subject in the context of the churches I pastored, but it is important to understand the role of music in the context of a denomination or fellowship. This fact can hardly be overstated. What should unite us and bless us has been allowed to divide us and in some cases breed discord within the church. As already mentioned, leadership must use godly wisdom in knowing how to use contemporary music in order to maintain the unity of the Spirit. I found it very interesting to watch the national Music Department which was once very influential and productive become almost nonexistent. To put this subject in context, church music once anchored in hymnbooks and denominational influence was replaced by the worldwide appeal of gifted musicians and musical groups such as:  Bill Gaither, Carol Cymbala and the Brooklyn Tabernacle Choir, Darlene Zschech from Australia, and most recently the music produced by Bethel Church in Redding, California. As far as I can ascertain, all of it is anointed and powerful. The fact remains that the emergence and popularity of these different groups have contributed to our churches becoming less dependent on Headquarters in a vital area.

The second area of transformational change that is still evolving with some unintentional consequences is the growth of the mega church movement within the world of religion and the Assemblies of God in particular. In my thinking, most of the results are positive. For instance, the mega church is more effective in church planting than any national or district could ever be for obvious reasons. The mega church can give immediate and personal oversight to a new church plant. It is capable of supplying necessary resources with specificity. A personal friend of mine told me that he made a great mistake when he planted two very successful churches in his city to the point that both of them qualified to become sovereign churches; but when he removed his oversight, both pastors proceeded to "do their own thing" beyond the principles and authority of the church that planted them and the Assemblies of God, resulting in both churches failing. He has now mothered a number of churches in his area, but the mother church maintains strong oversight over all of them to the point where the senior pastors of those churches still attend staff meetings at the mother church. Before going to Springfield, I pastored a very strong church; but my approach to church planting was through district home missions. I can imagine if I were still pastoring Bethel, I would add church planting to our five-year plans. All of this new approach to church planting is lessening the need and influence of national and district home missions departments.

In most situations, the mega church produces bible studies and other material for their own church and the churches they plant. Many of these church plants have their own worship teams, but the sermon from the mother church is televised to all the satellite churches. Many mega churches have their own missions programs, children and youth camps, and even ministerial training centers in the local church. The list goes on and on with the result that their need for the programs and services offered from Headquarters and district offices becomes almost nonexistent. Because of technology, even the small church takes advantage not only of the music but also resources produced by other churches and religious organizations.

The third area of change in the Assemblies of God USA is difficult for me to accept, but the facts speak for themselves. There has been a steady decline in the number of people who have received the gift of the Holy Spirit with the initial evidence of speaking with other tongues. In other words, the Pentecostal churches I grew up in and pastored are losing their Pentecostal distinctive.

One of the main reasons is the fact that many of our churches have abandoned the traditional Sunday School which is not in and of itself a bad thing but in some situations there is no good alternative program offered to systematically teach the Word of God and some who do have such a program are using non-Pentecostal teaching materials. In many of our churches, a person could attend for years and think they were in an evangelical church. As a Pentecostal and a former executive with the Assemblies of God, I am very concerned that we are losing our hunger for the supernatural power of God in conviction of sin, divine healing, prophesy, and Spirit-anointed preaching. I am encouraged by a growing number of our pastors who are beginning to pray and believe for a revival of signs and wonders which made the Assemblies of God a unique church.

All of these things and more were forces at work in the Assemblies of God when the new Board of Administration assumed leadership in 1993. I will always be thankful for the privilege of working under the leadership of Thomas Trask, one of the finest Christian gentlemen I have ever met. He was a fervent Pentecostal and did his best through the years to fan the flames of true revival in the Assemblies of God. He had been the district superintendent of Michigan and then pastored a great church for many years in the city of Detroit. About the same time I came to Springfield as the director of the Decade of Harvest, Bro. Trask was elected general treasurer. Anyone who worked with him soon learned he was a financial genius. When he came to Headquarters, the operation was approximately $4 million in the red. Under his leadership, the operation was soon in the black and stayed that way as long as he was in office.

For decades the Gospel Publishing House had been the major source of funding for the Assemblies of God Headquarters. Many people still believe the tithes of the ordained ministers pay for the total operation of Headquarters including salaries, benefits, buildings and properties, etc. Such is not the case. The contribution of the ministers to Headquarters is minuscule. The districts require that most of the ministers' tithes go for their operation. Many of the districts ask for 100 percent of the ministers' tithes.

Bro. Trask saw that the demise of the Gospel Publishing House was inevitable because of the massive changes in printing and publishing through technology so he started the Assemblies of God Financial Services which was designed to invest ministers' retirement funds, provide church loans, and a myriad of other services. It has become one of the leading religious financial institutions in the world and is the major source of income to fund our Headquarters operation. One of my assignments as assistant general superintendent was to chair the committee that approved church loans over a million dollars. Bro. Trask taught me a very valuable lesson which was not only to accept change but also to use it to better serve the kingdom of God. Too many church organizations have fallen into the trap of believing that propping up nonproductive traditions and methods is more important than being effective agents of change which is another term for a productive faith.

In my opinion, religious organizations in general and the Assemblies of God in particular must never confuse the temporal (traditional) with the eternal and must learn to make dramatic changes without compromising eternal truth because the whole world is changing dramatically. The old ways of doing things are becoming less and less productive. It is always necessary to embrace change including new leadership because God brings people to the kingdom for "such a time as this." I am no longer a leader but now a cheerleader for a new generation because I am not equipped to lead a church in this "new world." For instance, I do not embrace nor am I comfortable with a lot of the new technology. The new generation of spiritual leaders speaks a new language and lives in a new culture, but with those changes comes a new responsibility to contend for the faith once delivered to the saints.

Allow me to get ahead of myself for a few minutes. Bro. Trask and the Board of Administration who served with him made some dramatic changes in how the Assemblies of God operates and functions, but I cannot imagine the changes that will need to be made by new leadership in order to remain relevant. For instance, the structure and operation of Headquarters face inevitable change. Even when I was in office, my role or assignments changed dramatically. I was asked to give oversight to departments and ministries which had traditionally demanded full-time or part-time executive directors. By the end of my last term in office, I chaired or served on 42 boards and committees. I mention this only to illustrate the rapid changes that happened in just 14 years, but those changes that were made will pale in comparison to the inevitable changes that are on the horizon for the "new" Assemblies of God.

Do not be surprised that in the near future fewer and fewer people will work at Headquarters. A number of years ago there were over 1,000. That number has already dropped by several hundred because of technology. Do not be surprised if many districts will soon be led by pastors instead of full-time district superintendents. Do not be surprised if districts will be realigned and become more regional in administration. Do not be surprised if more of our resident colleges and universities will merge or close because of online education.

My years serving as the assistant general superintendent were very rewarding. I was given two of the finest executive secretaries at Headquarters. First was Shelley Mackey who was "stolen" from me by the general superintendent's office. She was replaced by Jackie Chrisner who was equally professional and gifted. They did an amazing job in keeping me "on track" which was not always easy. They answered my phone, kept my calendar, typed my sermons, worked with the travel agencies to get the best flights possible plus a hundred other duties all the while becoming "honorary" members of our family. I had no idea as a pastor how many exceptional people worked at Headquarters. As far as I could ascertain, every person with whom I worked was professional, pleasant, committed to Christ, and involved in their local church. They are probably the most unappreciated, dedicated large group of people anywhere in the world.

One of the interesting aspects of my assignment as the assistant general superintendent was to represent the Assemblies of God and to work with a wide range of other Pentecostal and evangelical churches and denominations. Our Board of Administration met annually with the leaders of the Canadian Assemblies. The fact that I was born in Canada opened doors to preach at their General Council and in many of their churches. The Pentecostal Assemblies of Canada is almost exactly 10 percent of the size of the Assemblies of God in the U.S. reflecting the same percentage of population between both countries.

In 2007, Ramona and I traveled to Indonesia to take part in a marvelous conference attended by over 2,700 ministers. I had the privilege of being teamed up with Jack Hayford of the Foursquare Church, Bishop Jerry Macklin of the Church of God in Christ, and three of the leading Indonesian pastors. I mention this to illustrate what a tremendous impact Pentecost has had around the world. I had no idea how strong the Pentecostal church had become in places we once considered "closed to the gospel."

Our leadership in the Assemblies of God maintains good communication and strong links to almost all Pentecostal denominations and organizations. For several years I served as the president of the Pentecostal

Fellowship of North America (now known as the Pentecostal Charismatic Churches of North America). I also represented the Assemblies of God on a committee consisting of well-known Charismatic leaders such as Kenneth Copeland, Oral Roberts, Billy Joe Daugherty, and several others. In addition, I had the opportunity to meet from time to time with the leadership of the Church of God in Cleveland, Tennessee (not to be confused with the non-Pentecostal Church of God in Anderson, Indiana), and the Foursquare Church.

We also met on occasion with the leadership of the Southern Baptist Convention. I learned very quickly their organization was far different from ours. For instance, their top leader was not a full-time general superintendent but one of their leading pastors who remained the pastor of his church. His role was basically ceremonial. Their executive leadership with whom we met from time to time was their National Sunday School Board. Bro. Trask was in the top leadership of the National Association of Evangelicals.

Surprisingly, one of the most delightful relationships I built over the years was with the Church of God in Christ. I was honored to preach in the church of the presiding bishop of New York on several occasions. They enjoyed Ramona's piano playing so much they invited her to give a full concert.

All my life, starting with Dr. Leonard Heroo, I have always enjoyed and appreciated black preachers, many of whom are great orators. I delighted in their ability to be so descriptive and graphic in telling a story, like the black preacher who was preaching about Gideon. He said, "The man of God was hiding behind a rock eating lunch and hiding from the enemy. Suddenly, the angel of the Lord came down and the man of God, he scared. He said, 'You be for us or against us?' and the angel of the

Lord said, 'I'm not here to choose up sides; I be here to take ovah.'"

In 1995, I flew on the company plane to Memphis, Tennessee, to represent the Assemblies of God at the funeral of the presiding bishop of the Church of God in Christ, Bishop William Henry Ford as Bro. Trask was ministering overseas. One of the reasons why it was important for the Assemblies of God to have an official representative at the funeral was because our churches shared a common Pentecostal history. Prior to 1914 when the Assemblies of God was officially established, Pentecostal people worshipped together. Historians are not agreed on the reasons why the Church of God in Christ and the Assemblies of God decided to form their own fellowships; but the fact remains the separation seemed amicable, and to this day the leaders of both organizations maintain a good relationship.

Several thousand filled the auditorium for the funeral of Bishop Ford. As far as I could tell, I was one of only three white men who were present. I was seated on the side of the platform facing Jesse Jackson. Every 10 minutes two "guards" would march to the coffin and replace the two who had been standing at attention. It was probably the grandest funeral I have ever witnessed. The eulogy was given by his successor, Bishop Owens; and I still remember it. It is worth sharing. He came to the pulpit and said words to this effect:

As great a heavyweight champion as Mike Tyson may be, he is not my champion. It took Mike Tyson 10 rounds to become the heavyweight champion of the world, but it only took my Champion four rounds to become the heavyweight Champion of death. For the first round, my Champion ran everyone out of the room where the dead girl lay and said, "Honey, why don't you just get on up"; and when she did, my Champion said, "I do believe I have just won the first round."

The devil said, "She was barely warm. If I could get one on the way to the grave, I could win the second round." My Champion said, "I'll meet you there." They were taking the young man to the grave when Jesus stopped the funeral procession and said, "Young man, why don't you just get on up"; and when he did, my Champion said to the contender, "I do believe I have just won round two." The devil, he was mad. He said, "If I could get one who is in the grave, I could win the third round." Jesus said, "I'll meet you anytime and any place." Word came that Lazarus was dying and they called for Jesus to come quickly, but Jesus said, "It's way too early." On the third day Jesus met Martha who cried, "If you had been here, my brother would not have died!" Jesus said, "Your brother will rise again." Martha answered, "I know he will rise at the resurrection." Jesus said, "I am the resurrection!" Then my Champion walked up the 21 steps to the tomb and said, "Move that stone; and when they did, He said, "Lazarus, why don't you come on out of there"; and when he did, all wrapped up in grave clothes, Jesus said, "Loose him and let him go," and then turned to the devil and said, "I do believe I have just won round three." Then the devil said, "If I could just get my boney hands on Him, I would be the heavyweight champion of death; and Jesus said, "I'll meet you there, and you can even watch me die." It was then the devil made his greatest mistake, but for three days it looked like Satan was the new Champion of death. But on the third morning in the darkness of the tomb, a hand began to tremble, then reached up to remove the cloth that covered His face, stood to His feet, carefully folded the graveclothes because He would not need them anymore, and said, "Move that stone!" He then proceeded to step out into the light of a new morning and declared, "I am He that liveth and am alive forevermore, and I have just won the fourth round and am the undisputed Champion of death!"

When Bishop Owens said those words, he took out a big white napkin, threw it toward the widow and walked away. By that time, the whole crowd, including myself, was on their feet praising God.

It was my privilege to attend the Pentecostal World Conference in Seoul, Korea, with the Board of Administration and to lead in prayer at the stadium filled with over 100,000 believers. Pastor Cho had told me earlier that he had wanted to build a church stadium to seat 50,000 at a time but the Lord told him to start new churches instead. From time to time, he would tell 10,000 people who attended the mother church living in a defined area of the city they were to go to the new church, and they did. Can you imagine starting a new church in a new location and having 10,000 members the first Sunday? It was interesting to attend one of the services at the mother church. Thousands of people would crowd into the auditorium and begin to pray with loud voices. When it was time for the service to begin, a bell would ring and the crowd would suddenly become quiet. The music was rather formal and the sermon comparatively short. The crowd would be dismissed and go out exits to the sides while thousands poured in from the back of the auditorium to begin praying until the next service started. They did that seven times a Sunday.

Another memorable trip I took was with Bro. Trask to Russia before the fall of the wall. I was amazed at the spiritual intensity of those believers. Some years before I took that trip, Ramona and I had journeyed to Florida to take our first Caribbean cruise to celebrate our twenty-fifth wedding anniversary. The cruise was scheduled to leave late on Sunday afternoon; and since we did not have a car, I decided to walk a few blocks and see if I could slip into a church service. Down the street from our hotel, I spotted a magnificent church building and was pleased to see the service was scheduled to begin in just a few minutes. When I walked in, I was more than impressed by the size and beauty of the sanctuary which had to seat well over 1,000 people. The platform was bedecked with bouquets of fresh flowers. The service began with the sound of a great pipe organ and four ministers took their places on the platform. I glanced at the church bulletin and read their names and noted three of them were listed as PhDs and the "uneducated" one only had a master's degree. After we had sung a couple of hymns, we heard a beautiful song sung by a well-trained sextet who had been sitting to the side of the platform. The minister gave a very fine 20-minute sermon from the book of Proverbs. The most startling thing about the entire service was the fact that by sitting near the back I was able to count exactly 62 people in the audience. The bulletin invited all of us to a postservice brunch in one of the side halls. I had to attend for two reasons. First, I thought the food would be good; and second, I had to ask why the crowd was so small. Three of the ministers were there, but I chose to get in conversation with the young "uneducated" one. I said to him, "Sir, I have been a pastor of a church in California and I have to ask you how you can support a highly educated staff and maintain such a magnificent church building with so few people?" I will never forget how he swelled up with pride and said, "We are so well-endowed we would have no trouble operating the church like it is for the next hundred years." For some reason those words came back to me with clarity when I sat in a church in Moscow after walking down an alley into a warehouse that would seat around 400 but was crammed full of at least 600, some standing around the perimeter for the whole service with children and youth sitting on the floor at the front. The place did not smell like fresh flowers and had no stained-glass windows or professional singers, but the whole atmosphere was charged with the presence of God as those Russians lifted their voices in praise. The thought occurred to me that "this church is so well-endowed they can worship like this for the rest of eternity."

Two weeks before I flew to India to preach their national conference which would be held in Madras-Chennai, I was walking out the door of a motel in Amarillo, Texas, holding two heavy suitcases unaware there had been an ice storm during the night and proceeded to have my feet slip out from under me and land on my lower back on the edge of a concrete step. It was a miracle Ramona and I were able to make the flight back to Springfield where I had x-rays taken. The doctor told me that without question if I had fallen an inch or two higher on my back, I would have been paralyzed for life or perhaps killed.

On the flight to India, I began to suffer some discomfort in my lower back but was able to function normally for several days. My itinerary was quite full. It is typical of foreign leaders to fill every minute of a guest's visit with activities and preaching assignments. In addition to preaching the conference at night, I was taken to see the sights in Madras-Chennai, a city of close to 5 million people. I was asked if I would be willing to meet the pastor of a comparatively new church in a poor part of the city. Of course, I readily agreed to do so. I was taken in a van down several streets until we ran out of paved road. We walked down a poorly maintained dirt road and was told to keep to the left side because an open sewer ran along the right side. We turned a corner and came to the church which consisted of a concrete slab (no chairs) and a roof. The pastor, wearing newly pressed pants and a clean white shirt, stood proudly by his wife dressed in her finest waiting to greet me. It was all I could do to hold back the tears. They told me their story. He had been a successful businessman, and God had called him to leave his business and start this church. He told me how God had performed miracle after miracle, the most dramatic being the salvation of a witch doctor who had previously held spiritual control of the neighborhood. His wife then told me that she held a bible study for women once a week which was running close to 300 at the church (sitting on concrete). The pastor told me they were believing God to be able to add to the building which would allow them to nearly double their attendance, but it was going to cost over $3,000. You can be sure I told them I would make certain they would get the money within 60 days, and I did.

Three days after arriving in India, the pain in my back worsened and became so excruciating I remember trying to get some relief by rocking back and forth on the edge of a table in my hotel room the day before I was to return to Springfield. It is nothing short of a miracle that I was able to stand and preach to thousands of people that day with no pain; but the minute I walked off the platform, the pain returned and increased to the point I had to ask Pastor Mohan if he could recommend a doctor to help me. It came as a bit of a shock when he told me there were approximately 150 medical doctors who attended the church and said, "I'll send one of the best to your hotel as soon as I can." A young doctor did come and told me to lie down on the bed. He took my right foot and lifted my leg about two feet off the bed without a problem. He then took my left foot and started raising my leg when I let out a loud groan before he hardly got it an inch off the bed. He said, "There's the problem." I felt like telling him I already knew that. He prescribed three different kinds of pain pills to get me home. The total cost of the prescriptions was $3.20. The doctor at home told me he would have prescribed the same three drugs. When I told him what I had paid, he said tongue in cheek, "Reverend, I call that a pretty good deal." I ultimately had to have surgery to remove bone chips that had worked their way into my nerve center as a result of the fall. According to my surgeon, I was fully recovered about six weeks sooner than normal.

During my tenure as assistant general superintendent, I visited the White House on two occasions. The first time while serving as the director of the Decade of Harvest, Ramona and I joined all of the assistant district superintendents and their wives for their annual meeting which was held that year in Washington, D.C. One of the leaders of the organization was Bobby Johnson who pastored a great church in Arkansas where Bill Clinton had visited from time to time when he was the governor. He liked to join the orchestra at the church sometimes to play his saxophone. When Bobby told the President we were coming to Washington, he told Bobby he would be very pleased to greet us. On a given day, we all gathered in the Rose Garden and waited for the President to return from a speaking engagement in the city. It was quite a sight to watch the motorcade pull in and see the President walk toward us. He was more than charming (he liked my tie). He addressed the group with his hand resting on Ramona's shoulder for most of the time. She told us she was not going to ever wash it again but then changed her mind after the scandal broke.

During the second term of George W. Bush, he requested that Bro. Trask and I come to the White House to meet with him. I was quite surprised how quickly and easily we passed through security. When we were told to go to the Oval Office, the President himself greeted us. He was very casual, first explaining that the rug in the center of the room had been chosen by Laura; and then he said, "Let's get the pictures out of the way," and seemingly from out of nowhere, a photographer appeared and proceeded to take a picture of Bro. Trask and President Bush and then did the same with me. We settled down on the couches to talk. I believe the main reason he wanted to speak to us was that he had some questions about

how to best address moral issues, especially homosexuality and other difficult subjects. At the end of our half-
hour meeting, his chief of staff signaled we should end
the meeting. Bro. Trask requested I pray for the president
before we left, and I was honored to do so.

In 1994, Bro. Trask spoke to Ramona and told her he
was very concerned about many small churches who did
not have suitable altar music of any kind and asked her
if she and Dixie Hackett would produce a recording that
would be a blessing for churches with limited resources.
I do not think he realized that he had given birth to an
idea that would be so effective. Ramona, playing the
piano, and Dixie, playing the organ, produced the first
recording (a cassette tape at the time) entitled "Music
for the Altar." It was so well-received they followed soon
after with "Music for the Anointing." After almost 30 years,
churches and individuals are still buying those recordings (now CDs). We received a report some time ago
that a Catholic church in Missouri uses them on a regular
basis. Ramona went on to produce several more CDs
on her own.

Through the years, the Lord has not only used Ramona's wonderful musical ability but she has also been an
effective speaker on her own at women's conferences
and other venues. One time she returned from a speaking
engagement and told me she had a very unique experience at an airport. For one of the few times in her life,
she decided to save money by rolling her suitcase to
the gate to save tipping someone to help her. To tell you
the truth, I think she could not find a porter. She headed
for the nearest escalator to go up to the gate and was
doing all right until she realized too late that her suitcase was too wide for the escalator. When the luggage
hit both sides of the escalator and would not go through, it
yanked Ramona backwards and she landed on the escalator shelf with her feet in the air. Of course, the escalator

kept moving and took her purse and shoes on up but left her flailing away with no traction to allow her to stand. Her luggage stayed behind her. Two airport employees were able to help her, and she wound up tipping both of them. She will be forever grateful she was wearing slacks and not a dress. Sometimes it is very expensive to try and save money.

During our years in Springfield, ten of our grandchildren were born. Three of them, Brittney Byerley, Rylie Silva, and Morgan Roncone, were born six weeks apart in February, April, and June. When those three babies were under seven months old, they were all taken to the General Council in Portland, Oregon, and caused quite a sensation. We had so many grandchildren so fast that some called us "the rabbit family." I just think they were jealous.

We were pretty excited when we learned that our oldest daughter, Renee, who had already given us two beautiful grandchildren, Blake and Brittney, was going to have twins. Little did we know what she was about to go through. Early in her pregnancy, our whole family decided to take the opportunity to spend a week together in a very large cabin of a friend in Colorado. We were all having a wonderful time when Renee suddenly took ill; and it looked like if we did not get her to a hospital, she would lose the babies. The closest hospital was about 25 miles from the cabin so because of the distance, we called the Highway Patrol and told them we were on our way but would need to go way over the speed limit. They said, "Okay, we'll let everyone know you're coming but be careful." It was quite a ride. My son-in-law, David Byerley, was driving 100 miles an hour on some stretches; and I was praying all the way that she would make it, that the babies would be spared, and that David would not lose control of the car. All three of those prayers were answered, and we continued our vacation with very grateful hearts. But that was just the beginning of trouble.

The twins were born very premature with Brandon weighing 2 lbs. 9 ozs. and Brady 2 lbs. 2 ozs. The babies had to be taken early because Renee would have died of toxemic poisoning. At the time, David and Renee were ministers of music at Tommy Barnett's Dream Center in the Los Angeles area. When the twins were born, they were taken to Cedars Sinai Medical Center where they stayed for three months. During those months, David and Renee took a music position at a church in Houston, Texas; but the need for Brandon to have heart surgery when he grew to five pounds hung heavy in our own hearts. While we were at the 1995 General Council in St. Louis, we received word Brandon needed to have surgery to save his life. It was a happy moment when we received word that the surgery was a success; but in less than an hour, David called to tell us that as the surgeon was removing the catheter, he punctured his heart. We faced the real possibility we could lose little Brandon. As Ramona prepared to fly to Houston, the entire General Council of several thousand believers prayed for Brandon.

That evening Ramona arrived in Houston. Brandon was in very critical condition, and the medical staff did not give the family much hope. Late that night Ramona and Renee went to the hotel for a few hours' sleep. When they returned to the hospital early the next morning, the attending nurse was all smiles. She said, "I went to check Brandon's vitals about 3 o'clock this morning and was thrilled that the heart was beginning to pump on its own and all his vitals had greatly improved. Then I got a light to look into his eyes and almost shouted 'There's life there!'" Today Brandon is finishing his fourth year of study at Northpoint Bible College to prepare for the ministry. Brady is finishing his second year in the Boston area in a very fine school for special needs students. It was very touching to me when I heard that when the twins were born, Renee affixed a scripture to each of the boy's incubators in the ICU unit. The scripture on Brandon's crib was "I shall not die, but live, and declare the works of the        " (Psalm 118:17 KJV). Brady's scripture was "'For I know the plans I have for you,' declares the L       , 'plans to prosper you and not to harm you, plans to give you hope and a future'" (Jeremiah 29:11 NIV).

Our children and grandchildren have been a pure delight, and I will need to write another book telling about them. I know it will be an immediate best seller because most people love to hear the few grandparents who are willing to share about how beautiful and talented their grandchildren are. One great memory stands out in my mind when they were small and everyone had come to our home in Springfield to celebrate Christmas with us. Ramona arranged for a retired minister she had heard about to come to the house dressed up like Santa Claus. I will never forget the looks of wonder on the faces of the little ones and what fun we had. She had prearranged for him to have one gift designated for each grandchild. They were so in awe of it all. The reason the evening was so special for all of us was that just before he left, he sat down and read the Christmas story.

In 2006, I began to feel my role as assistant general superintendent should be finished at the next General Council, and at the same time, I knew I should not retire even though I would be turning 70. I went to the 2007 Council not knowing what the Lord had in mind for my future. I did not think that at my age I should let my name stand in the voting for a new general superintendent; but at the same time, I was not sure if the Lord wanted me to serve one term as a bridge between a new generation of leaders. I was a bit relieved when the Council elected George O. Wood and released me from national leadership. However, I came back to Springfield a bit conflicted. On the one hand, I wanted to retire and remain in our very beautiful home that included my incredible study and library containing almost 10,000 volumes; but on the other hand, I had that nagging, irritating feeling I would not be retiring for another few years.

During the General Council, Dennis Marquardt, the district superintendent of Northern New England, asked me if I would be willing to consider becoming the new president of Zion Bible College outside of Providence, Rhode Island. For many reasons, it was one of the least desirable possibilities I had ever considered which makes it a rather interesting story.

In 1924, Christine Gibson, a close friend of my father's and mother's mentioned in the Chapter 2 of this book, founded the School of the Prophets in East Providence, Rhode Island. They later changed the name to Mt. Zion School of the Prophets; and when I first became aware of the school, it was called Zion Bible Institute.

For many years, Zion taught and trained most of the independent Pentecostal ministers throughout the northeast and New Brunswick, Canada. A good number of our Assemblies of God ministers are also alumni. The centerpiece of the campus was Zion Gospel Temple that exists to this day. The campus itself consisted primarily of two-story homes converted to dorms; but over the years, it became quite clear the school needed a more adequate campus and a safer environment in order to attract and keep more students. The school also desired to become a fully accredited college which was a practical impossibility in a deteriorating neighborhood setting, a number of faculty without qualifying degrees, an inadequate library, and very little money.

In 1985 under the leadership of a new president, Dr. Benjamin Crandall, Zion was able to purchase the 200-acre Barrington College in the city of that same name for only $5 million. Dr. Crandall wrote an interesting book giving an account of how they overcame powerful opposition from the town that wanted the property to move away from a nonprofit status for tax purposes, the accrediting association with its religious bias, and the banks that did not want to loan money to a college with no financial resources. It is obvious God wanted Zion to survive and performed several miracles to make it happen, but the road ahead would prove to be difficult.

In order to bring the debt down to a manageable size, Zion had to sell large parcels of land to developers. That was accomplished rather quickly; however, the college still faced two very large financial challenges in order to function effectively. The Barrington campus was large with more than enough buildings to meet Zion's needs, but most of them were badly out of code requiring everything from new sprinkler systems to handicap access and the list went on and on. Apart from the building codes, many of the buildings needed significant repairs—in some cases, new roofs, heating and air conditioning, and road repairs not to mention basic upkeep such as flooring and painting.

The second financial challenge was the comparatively small enrollment for such a large physical campus coupled with the necessity to keep tuition costs low in order to be competitive. By its very definition, a bible school training students for ministry does not attract too many students with adequate financial resources. Most churches struggled with their own budgets and historically gave more to foreign missions than to higher education. In Zion's situation, the number of Pentecostal churches in the region was quite small. It was a wise decision in the year 2000 to bring the college under the auspices of the Assemblies of God because it opened the door for more students and church support. However, a larger AG school called Valley Forge Christian College in Pennsylvania was attracting many students from the northeast resulting in very real competition between the two colleges.

By the year 2013 when I left the national office, Zion Bible College was in rather dire straits.

I have intentionally outlined the reasons why I had no interest in accepting the offer to even consider becoming the president, especially at age 70. In my thinking, no rational person of any age would want to jump into the middle of what appeared to be an impossible situation.

Now I am ready to tell you what the famous radio personality, Paul Harvey, used to say, "the rest of the story." As I have said, I had turned down the possibility of becoming the president after "retirement" and thought I had made myself quite clear. Not long after, the chairman of Zion's board, Robert Wise, the superintendent of the Southern New England District, asked me to reconsider; and my answer to him was a definite "no." I thought the matter was settled until I called my sister, Hazel, the wife of Bob Hoskins. The following conversation took place: "Hazel, you will never believe what the guys up in New England asked me to do. Bob Wise just called and asked me to consider becoming the president of Zion." I will confess I was chuckling about it. I thought because of our family attachment to Zion in the past, she would get a kick out of the idea. I waited a bit for her response to the point I thought I had lost our connection. Then she said, "You know, you ought to do it. Zion started out as an independent Pentecostal school with Sis. Gibson. You and I grew up with Zion and know all about it. Now it is Assemblies of God, and I think you are uniquely qualified because I can't think of anyone who knows both the independents and the Assemblies of God like you do." My answer to her was not very spiritual. I said, "I think you're crazy," and soon ended the conversation.

About two days after my conversation with Hazel, she called me back and said, "Charles, I'm serious. I really feel you should be the president of Zion." I said, "Hazel, I'm serious. I do not want to be the president or anything else to do with Zion. You have no idea what a mess they are in." She said, "What would it take to change your mind?" I said, "The audible voice of God might help or an undeniable sign." That is all she needed to hear. I suddenly realized I had had about the same conversation with Glen Cole who had decided I should become the director of the Decade of Harvest initially against my will.

About a month after I had shut the door on Zion, I was shocked to hear that David Green, the owner of the Hobby Lobby stores, had purchased the historic Bradford College campus for an undisclosed amount of money and was going to gift it to Zion. I called him and said, "David, what are you doing?" He answered and said, "Hazel told me if I bought Bradford and gave it to Zion, you would be the president." Very few times in my life have I ever been speechless; but on this occasion, I was without words for several seconds. I did not want to be the president and, at the same time, did not want to ruin the purchase for Zion so I said, "But David, that's an old campus. I bet it would take millions to bring it up to code." I was thinking of the Bradford campus and knew it must have been 100 years older than the one Zion occupied. He said, "Oh, I know that. We'll get right to work on it and have it ready for you to open in the fall."

The history of Bradford College is rather interesting. It was established in Bradford, Massachusetts (now Haverhill), in 1803 as Bradford Academy, a coeducational institution. It is fascinating to me in light of what happened in 2007 that it had become known as a center for the training of missionaries. In 1836, it chose to become exclusively a women's college which it was for the next 135 years when it again became coeducational. In 2000, it closed its doors because of massive debt and declining enrollment. It had been in operation on the same campus for 197 years. For the next 7 years it sat dormant and the buildings fell into almost total disrepair. A commercial development firm had purchased the entire campus and recouped their investment cost by building houses and condos on over half the property which were once ball-fields and other sports facilities. When they wanted to dismantle the main buildings of the campus to put up more commercial buildings, the town fathers refused their building permits because they had designated many of the original buildings as historical landmarks. The owners did everything in their power to destroy the buildings such as refusing to fix leaking roofs and turning the heat off in the dead of winter so the pipes would burst in order to ultimately get a permit to go ahead with their plans. During that period of time, I learned that a group of evangelical Christians would have regular prayer walks around that old campus praying that God would somehow use Bradford College again as a training institution for ministers and missionaries as it had 150 years before. God heard those prayers and preserved the campus for His purpose.

The restoration of Bradford College was more than remarkable. David Green told me that for six months he had over 100 builders, craftsmen, technicians, land-scapers, and decorators working to get the campus ready for Zion to move from Rhode Island to Haverhill in time to start the fall semester in 2007; and he did it. The renovations cost Hobby Lobby over $5 million. In the five years I served as president, David Green gave $3 million personally to help us with operations. He only visited the college one time, but his wife Barbara served faithfully on our trustee board. She remains heavily involved in the college. According to David, one of the main reasons they were so interested in helping Zion was because it was the only accredited college in the Assemblies of God that required every student to be a Bible major.

It was more than interesting when he personally showed Ramona and me the beginnings of his collection of ancient Bible manuscripts and other related books and materials which would fill the incredible Museum of the Bible in Washington, D.C., costing over a billion dollars. On another occasion he told us that when he first started Hobby Lobby, they were very successful; but through a period of setbacks, they faced bankruptcy. It was at that time God spoke to him and made clear the reason for the failure was because he thought it belonged to David Green; but if he would begin operating the company with God as the owner and using all the profits by divine direction, the business would prosper and grow. When I would thank him for his contribution to Zion, he would always say in different ways that he was only investing God's money, not his. The Greens have certainly been a blessing to many ministries but especially to my sister and me. They have poured millions of dollars into One Hope, once called the Book of Hope which was founded by my brother-in-law, Bob Hoskins. The anniversary celebration for One Hope was held at the Museum of the Bible before it was officially opened to the public. I cannot begin to imagine the crowns they will receive when they enter heaven, but I am sure they will lay them all down at the feet of the Master with great expertise because they have been doing it for so many years here on earth.

My installation as president of Zion Bible College took place on the Barrington, Rhode Island, campus. For me, it was more than an official event; it was a moment filled with emotions and memories. I was becoming the president of the school founded by Christine Gibson, the woman who knelt before me as a little boy and said, "Now Charles, you get ready to be a man of God." I know she is in heaven, but she was at my installation in a very real way. Memories of my father preaching at Zion while Sister Gibson and Dr. Heroo were serving as presidents came flooding back. In the audience sat Dr. Benjamin Crandall, the president God used to move Zion from East Providence to Barrington. A whole delegation of people came all the way from Headquarters in Springfield, Missouri, to be present. The "new" friends I would work with for the next five years including the entire Board of Trustees, the Board of Administration, the faculty, and most of the staff were in the audience; and then all of us sat back to listen to Dr. Thomas E. Trask, the former general superintendent and my good friend and former "boss," give a powerful challenge exhorting Zion and me to keep the faith, stay Bible-centered and remain thoroughly Pentecostal. The greatest emotions I felt were peace and joy because I knew Ramona and I were in the perfect will of God. I certainly knew we were not in it for the money. I agreed to take a salary in order to help maintain a realistic budget for accounting purposes and future administrations with the understanding I would return half to the college for operations and use the other half for our housing allowance.

One very big hurdle we faced before opening the doors to the Haverhill campus was to gain accreditation by the State of Massachusetts in order to grant degrees. Everyone knows that Massachusetts is a very liberal state, and that fact is compounded many times over in their world of higher education. Many people told me it would be most unusual if we were granted full accreditation because there was such a bias against evangelicals, let alone Pentecostals. We made our appeal a very focused and intense matter of prayer. It would be difficult to express the feelings of our Board of Administration as we made our way to Boston to meet with the State Board of Education. Personally, I would express my feelings as more concern than fear. We were all genuinely surprised by the warm welcome we received from those very liberal officials. After a few questions, our request for accreditation was approved. The Lord certainly gave us favor. I got the sense they were a bit proud of themselves that they were so broad-minded they would give accreditation to an evangelical/Pentecostal, single-focused bible college, the only one like it in the state. I must give a great deal of credit to our dean, Dr. Pat Gallagher, who is, in my mind, one of the greatest authorities in the country on matters concerning accreditation for Christian colleges. He had worked hard behind the scenes to anticipate all the concerns and requirements demanded by the state; and his effort, with the help of the Lord, paid off handsomely.

The five years we spent at Zion were packed with activity. Ramona never worked so hard in her life. Because of the financial situation at the college, she offered to work as my executive secretary without pay. In her case, we got a lot more than we paid her. When she had first worked as a secretary before we were married, she had one of the early electric typewriters, a mimeograph machine, and was proficient in shorthand. The first computer was nowhere on the horizon. She deserves a lot of credit for learning how to use a computer and rely on cell phones. She did have some of our technicians come in every other day or so to show her how to do something or fix a glitch of some kind. Besides working full time in the office, she traveled with me almost every weekend, attended most daily chapels, and delighted in having four of her grandchildren and some of their friends over to the house for dinner. She also took the minutes for the Board of Trustees and the Board of Administration. I have no idea how she was able to do it all.

One early evening after cooking dinner for the family, including our grandchildren, Ramona experienced pain and swelling in her lower leg. We took her immediately to the emergency room, and they in turn rushed her to a Boston hospital by ambulance where they determined she had blood clots in both legs and both lobes of the lungs. She was in the hospital for five days but experienced a miraculous recovery and was back at work within days. I often wondered if the Lord had arranged a time of rest for her. Seriously, Ramona was one of the main reasons I was able to enjoy leading Zion.

In addition to Ramona's "close call," I was also surprised to learn after one of my annual checkups that I had prostate cancer. The doctor gave me five choices for treatment. I chose to have surgery immediately. I was blessed to have one of the most gifted cancer specialists in the Boston area which means he was world-class. When I was wheeled into the operating room, one of the last things I saw was some of the brightest lights on a small area in the middle of the room.

When I awoke in my room later, I learned the surgeon was not even in the operating room but did the whole operation by remote control from another room in the hospital. He told me it was much safer and quicker and my recovery time would be shorter. He did tell us that my diagnosis had put my cancer on a scale of 5 in seriousness. During the surgery, he discovered it was at 9 and was attached to the wall of the lining of the prostate gland which, if the cancer had gone through that lining, would have gone into the bones of the spine. I am still thankful to God He impressed me to have surgery. To add to my gratitude, the surgeon was almost certain I would need some follow-up treatments; but as time went on, it was clear no further treatments would be necessary. As a side note, I will always be grateful that our district superintendent and chairman of Zion's board, Robert Wise, took a whole day out of his busy schedule to stay with Ramona and the family throughout the entire ordeal.

The tremendous amount of money given by David Green and Hobby Lobby was almost 100 percent for renovation with very little for operations. It is not my intention to bore my readers with unnecessary details, but the miracle of Zion cannot be appreciated without understanding the financial pressures we faced as an administration after the move to Haverhill. First of all, the old campus in

Barrington would not sell. There were too many problems facing potential buyers in the same way Zion had faced on the Bradford campus; but in our case, we had a donor with very deep pockets who was willing to pour millions into bringing the campus up to code and believed in our mission. For almost three years, Zion had to maintain the Barrington campus at a cost of many thousands of dollars a year. The costs included such things as security, mowing lawns, paying energy bills, snow removal to keep driveways open in case of emergency and the list goes on and on. We finally had to auction off the campus and realized less than a million dollars.

Even though the enrollment grew significantly at Zion, there was an annual shortfall of around $700,000. That problem met me every morning at my office door. Do not let anyone fool you; the president of a Christian college has to raise a lot of money. The highest degree education offers is no help when bills have to be paid, and the hardest money to raise is to pay for operations. Capital campaigns are a lot more glamorous and appealing; and in many cases, a professional fund-raiser can be quite effective. It is easier to motivate a potential donor to give toward a new building than to help pay health benefits or fix a furnace so my approach had to be much different. Here again my family helped me. We paid my daughter, Rachel Silva, a stipend to go through the Assemblies of God church directory and contact the pastors of every sovereign church, district by district, and set up a phone appointment for me to talk to the pastor about the possibility of giving an undesignated gift to help Zion. Most weeks I spent 15 to 20 hours on the phone. To tell you the truth, I really enjoyed it. Rachel told me that she was able to set up a phone appointment on the average of every fifth call she made. I do believe my name recognition from being the assistant general superintendent for so many years was a real help. It is probably one of the reasons the Lord chose me to lead Zion in that period of their history.

The next thing that helped us financially was through a man named Ed Laughlin. Ed had been a very successful businessman and my brother David's church treasurer for many of the years David pastored First Assembly in Worcester, about 50 miles from Zion. Ed offered to come help me by running the Finance Office for almost nothing. He served as the treasurer for all the years I was president. He and his wife Shirley remain close friends. I attribute a great deal of my success as president directly to Ed Laughlin.

It would be difficult for me to give enough credit to Dr. Patrick Gallagher who served as the academic dean during my years at Zion. He was raised Roman Catholic; but during the Charismatic Renewal, his priest for some divine reason recommended he attend Zion. He remained at Zion after he graduated, joined the staff, earned his advanced degrees, became the dean at an early age, and has become known as the unofficial historian. He was my right-hand man in the area of academics. I could not have begun to administrate Zion without his love for God and the college and his expertise.

Near the end of my tenure at Zion, I was more successful at changing the name than I was when I tried to change Bethel to Winchester Cathedral. Even though the name Zion had not been a problem, I began to sense that it would probably be better to change the name of the school for a more contemporary generation who had no idea what the name Zion meant. Like Bethel, many from the outside thought Zion was some kind of a Jewish name so we changed the name to Northpoint Bible College. I was quite surprised at the little resistance we experienced to the name change in spite of the fact it had been called Zion for almost 90 years. The criticism that New

Englanders cannot change is not true. Just give them 90 years, and they might do it.

One of the things that made Zion such a wonderful training center was the daily chapels. It would be impractical to list the great guest preachers the students were privileged to hear day after day. They came from all over the country with the understanding we could not pay for their expenses or give them an honorarium; but they came anyway and many times brought significant amounts of money from their churches. It was certainly a win-win for us.

In addition to our guest preachers, I preached on the average of once a week. Every faculty member spoke once a semester as did seniors who had passed their homiletic course the semester before graduation.

Daily chapels provided music students an opportunity to develop their gifts as effective worship leaders. I have to admit I was a bit proud of myself for not demanding a certain kind of music because some of the new contemporary music does not seem to have a melody and is often louder than a siren; and by the time I begin to learn one, it is buried in the sea of forgetfulness never to be remembered anymore. I will admit I learned to like some of them and sometimes even now hum them under my breath so Ramona does not have to hear them. I gave freedom in the area of music with the understanding I had total control of the pulpit.

If a person lives a comparatively long life, it is inevitable they will outlive their parents and even siblings. In Ramona's case, she lost her mother Meda, whom I wrote about earlier in this book, when she was comparatively young. In 2003, she lost her father.

Ramona's father, Elmo J. Hudgins, who married my Aunt Gladys after the passing of Ramona's mother, was the quintessential Texan, genuine Pentecostal Christian, proud father, and musically gifted hard worker all in one.

Those who never met him missed meeting a delightful human being. His story is worth telling and remembering.

When Ramona was born, her mom and dad were so poor they lived in what was called a dugout which for all intents and purposes was a large shelter dug in the side of a hill. Elmo worked for a dollar a day (the same "salary" my dad made for several years) shoveling gravel and would be so exhausted he would have to lie down on the floor for a period of time before he could eat dinner. In spite of his financial poverty, he was rich in faith. When his wife, Meda, was pregnant with Ramona, she became sick and was diagnosed with tuberculosis and was told the baby she was carrying would be stillborn. Soon after a revival was held at their Assemblies of God church, an evangelist prayed for Meda. She was healed and delivered a beautiful baby girl who would become my wife 20 years later. At times, Ramona's parents did not have enough money to feed their new baby, but the local grocer trusted Elmo enough to give him milk on credit. He told me the family would walk to church in snow and rain, he with pieces of cardboard in his "holey" shoes carrying Ramona on his back. He was known to pray by the hour and never missed church in spite of their poverty. One night they discovered they had only one can of tomatoes left, but they believed God would somehow provide. The next morning, they walked out the door to find two large bags of groceries. They never did know whom God used to feed His faithful children.

God began to bless the Hudgins family for their faith and faithfulness. Not long after Ramona was born, Elmo got a better job and was able to buy his first house. In addition to buying his own house, he began to buy dilapidated houses, fix them up, and turn them into rental properties. He was one of the hardest workers I have ever known.

The story of Elmo Hudgins would not be complete without including the gift of music. Early in his marriage to Meda, the church they attended lost their pianist. Elmo told the Lord that if He would help him, he would teach himself to play for song service. He became a church pianist by learning shape notes and practicing. He became so good that some people would come to church just to watch him play. He and Meda had asked the Lord to give them a musically talented child. Ramona likes to say she can play the piano because the Lord saw fit to answer the prayers of her parents. Ramona began to pick out melodies on the piano at the age of four so piano lessons began and continued for the next 14 years. Of course, her parents were very proud of her and would always "show her off" by making her play for their guests. When she was about six, an evangelist and his wife were invited to the Hudgins' home for dinner; and of course, Ramona had to play the piano. They failed to tell her what to play so she began the great "hymn" with these inspirational words, "Pistol packin' mama, lay that pistol down, lay that pistol down, babe, lay that pistol down." From then on, I suspect they told her what to play.

Elmo had a wonderful, full life. He began to fail soon after Gladys, his second wife, died and went home to be with the Lord at the age of 89 in Fresno, California.

Soon after retiring to California, I lost my brother David who had been my big, brilliant, and funny older brother. When I was 13 years old, he went to Central Bible Institute, married Dawn McClure, and then began their ministries in St. John, New Brunswick, where they served as assistant pastors with Carro and Susie Davis for ten years. It always struck me as rather unique that my father and my older brother would work under the same spinster twins from Georgia.

Soon after Susie, one of the twins, died, David stayed on in St. John as a senior pastor. He had chosen not to get credentials with the Assemblies of God; but being the pastor of the largest Pentecostal church in all of the Atlantic provinces of Canada, he had great influence among many of the Pentecostal and evangelical churches, including the Assemblies of Canada. He started a very popular radio program called "Ask the Pastor." I was a guest on that program on several occasions; and since it was a live broadcast, you never knew what kind of odd question or weird caller would make the program for that day more than interesting.

David became a great preacher. His approach and style of preaching was quite different from mine. Whereas I did not take notes to the pulpit, he almost read his sermon from a small notebook he held in his hand. He did it so effectively the congregations were never distracted. His preaching helped me to teach homiletics and sermon preparation to hundreds of students through the years. I was able to use my brother as an example to prove no one's preaching style was superior to another. The key to effective Pentecostal preaching is prayerful prepara-tion before going to the pulpit and the anointing of the Holy Spirit in the pulpit. I have heard powerful anointed preaching from every kind of personality using every kind of preaching style imaginable. Some people have the idea that Pentecostal preaching must be loud and bom-bastic, but nothing could be further from the truth. I have heard the loud and the subdued, the proclaimer and the teacher, the extrovert and the introvert, the humorous and the serious, those who preach without notes and those who used extensive notes like my brother David. All could be effective.

When I left First Assembly in Des Moines to pastor Bethel Church, I was a bit surprised at how quickly David was asked to succeed me because he was not an Assem-blies of God credential holder which the constitution of the church required. Furthermore, you would think after having a Crabtree for over ten years, they would want some relief. David got his credentials almost overnight, and First Assembly flourished with "Crabtree the Second" for another ten years. During that time, the church built a beautiful new auditorium where the congregation still worships. David also became an executive presbyter and was chosen to preach at a General Council. It still amazes me how quickly he rose in the ranks of the Assemblies of God after being credentialed with them for such a short time.

The next and final church David and Dawn pastored was First Assembly of God in Worcester, Massachusetts, not far from Zion Bible College where he and Dawn taught once a week for several years in addition to their pastoral duties. The church grew as it had everywhere they pastored.

Several years after David moved to Worcester, we began to notice a change in his health. We were saddened to hear the news that he had been diagnosed with Parkinson's disease. He did very well for several years after the diagnosis but had to retire in 2008, the same year Ramona and I moved to Massachusetts to take the leadership of Zion.

David and Dawn retired in Florida for several reasons. The weather by all measures is better in Florida than Massachusetts as is the cost of living. Another plus was the fact they were able to move close to Hazel. I confess I learned to hate Parkinson's disease watching my brother slowly deteriorate from a strong healthy human being and delightful communicator to losing the ability to think clearly and move on his own. At the end of March 2014, he died at the age of 81.

For 68 years, we were brothers but only lived in the same house 13 of those years. I cannot count the number of times we had to say "good-bye." For 55 years, we never lived together in the same country and state, let alone the same house. People might think distance and time would make it impossible to have a close, meaningful relationship; but that is where they would be wrong. Distance is no barrier to love. Through the years, we had to say "good-bye" a lot, but that meant we had the privilege of saying "hello" a lot.

Let me tell you about our final "good-bye." I stood apart from the crowd in the middle of the street on March 30, 2014, in Boca Raton, Florida, and watched the back of the hearse carrying the physical remains of my brother quite quickly disappear from view. It was there (not the grave) where I said my final "good-bye."

Like many times before, he was "hitting the road"; but this time it was different. I knew I would never have to say "good-bye" to my brother again. In just a comparatively short time, I will see him again. I think I am going to yell, "We made it!" and whisper in his ear, "We'll never say 'good-bye' again!"

My sister Hazel was born in 1933, one and a half years after my brother David. Everyone should have known her. She was one of the most refreshing personalities I ever knew. She was one of the reasons I look back on my early childhood and smile because she was always making home a fun place to live. She became an outstanding pianist and unusually creative writer.

After graduating from high school in Bangor, Maine, she and my brother David attended CBI in Springfield, Missouri. After her college graduation, she moved to Sacramento, California, to be on the staff of the great Bethel Temple, now Capitol Christian Center, as a secretary and pianist. It was there she met Bob Hoskins, the young evangelist. After a long courtship, they were married in 1959 and proceeded to travel to Africa to begin their missionary careers. She wrote a book entitled *Honeymoon Safari*. I am almost certain no bride ever went through the first months of marriage in the same way Hazel did.

In spite of Hazel's great humor and zest for living, she was a deeply spiritual woman with an unusual prayer life and was a gifted speaker as well. When her three children were quite young, the whole family had to flee for their lives from Lebanon during a war there with only a couple of suitcases and the clothes on their backs. Later they settled in Florida, working at Life Publishers where they would begin the international ministry of what is now known as One Hope.

Hazel was always optimistic and made the best of every situation. She loved to tell of the time they were ministering in a Muslim country when a man came into the service and saw all the women with their heads covered. For some unknown reason, he got the idea he should cover his head as well, reached under his robe, pulled off his shorts, and stuck it on top of his head for the rest of the service.

One day, Hazel was sitting in the audience at a large conference where Bob was scheduled to minister. A woman came in and sat next to Hazel all excited about having the opportunity to hear the great Bob Hoskins. After gushing platitudes about Bob for a few minutes, she asked who Hazel was. When Hazel told her she was Bob Hoskins' wife, the lady just stared at her for a few seconds and said, "And you just sit there," so Hazel wrote her autobiography and titled it, *And I Just Sat There*. She was great.

In the spring of 2015, I am certain Hazel had some kind of a premonition she would not live long in spite of her overall good health. She told Bob they had to come to California to visit Ramona and me as well her younger sister Charlotte and her husband, Dr. Ray Carlson, who live in Redding, California, about a three-hour drive from Roseville. What a time we had, telling great stories, eating incredible food, and going down "memory lane." Bob told us later that her desk at home had always been a mess;

but soon after visiting us in California, she went home and put everything in place. Sure enough, on June 22, 2015, after a very brief illness of a few days, her heart gave out and she was taken from us at the age of 81, the same age David had been when he had died just a year and a half before. When Bob was asked if we should send memorial gifts in place of flowers, Bob told us Hazel had had an extraordinary love for flowers. I have never seen so many flowers in one place in my life. The whole front of the large church in Boca Raton was packed with gorgeous bouquets, a fitting tribute to a beautiful life. She was laid to rest next to her brother.

In writing this autobiography, I realized that the reader might get the impression I feel I have suffered an inordinate amount of loss and sorrow; but such is not the case. I have had the joy of being a member of a rare and delightful family for many, many years. Others might think my early life was miserable because of being raised in what many would call a radical Pentecostal home, church, and environment. I promise you, I have had a lot of fun. Others might think that living in New England is brutal because of the weather, but most of the time the change of seasons are worth a few weeks of snow and ice.

There were really some benefits living in New England as an adult. I say that because when I was growing up in Maine, I did not appreciate the history, culture, and beauty of that part of the world. Living in the Boston area as senior adults, we enjoyed taking guests to a myriad of historical sights. I really believe every American should experience the Freedom Trail. It is a little over two miles long with over a dozen historical "treasures" that stay in my mind such as The Boston Commons, Park Street Church, Kings Chapel, Old State House, Faneuil Hall, Paul Revere House, Old North Church, Bunker Hill Monument, and the USS Constitution, just to name a few.

We enjoyed visiting the Kennedy Library and the Bush summer home just over the border in Maine.

Allow me to give you just a taste of the incredible food available to the residents at all times and those "uncultured guests" who insist on visiting over and over but do not have enough sense to live there. All along the ocean up and down the coast, a person can sit by a lobster shack with their great boiling pots of water and be served a fresh whole lobster. No self-respecting New Englander would let anyone beside themselves break off the claws; take a nutcracker provided; crack open the claws and the tail; and then dip the savory, succulent, sweet, tender lobster meat in a small container filled with hot butter. I personally enjoyed having two of them as opposed to some who order one and add corn on the cob or a dish of fresh steamed clams. My theory is quite simple. If you are going to have lobster, then have lobster.

One of the greatest lobster eating experiences of my life happened when we chartered a small boat to go ocean fishing off the coast of Maine. In the middle of the day, the captain pulled to a dock on a small island where he invited us to disembark for lunch. He took us to a little cabin he owned and there served us the most delectable lobster stew I have ever had. It was so good I knew it had to be illegal and sure enough it was. The captain had kept several illegal lobsters which were under a pound from his catch of the day, taken the meat, added a little cream, butter, and salt and pepper and then served it to us piping hot.

After lobster, I enjoyed fresh clams and oysters. Right up there near the top is fresh haddock right out of the ocean. It is even better to go catch them yourself which we did from time to time. It took me some time to accept fresh cod as a very good fish because growing up, fresh brook trout, haddock, and salmon were far superior to cod. One time when we went fishing for haddock and cod,

I noticed Ramona must have hooked a big one because she was working so hard for so long to land it. When she finally brought it in, we all broke out laughing because there was not just one cod but two. She had hooked one in the mouth and then in her best Texan tradition had lassoed one by the tail. Some people accused her of telling a "tall tale," but several of us were there and watched her bring them in. There are ways to enjoy living in New England in spite of a little snow and ice from time to time.

We had decided to retire in Springfield, Missouri, and had purchased a beautiful lot on a golf course to build our home. One day out of the blue, Ramona said, "What do you think about retiring in the Sacramento area to be near Rachel (our middle daughter) and enjoy the California weather?" The idea appealed to me almost immediately, and we proceeded to have a new home built in a senior retirement development in Roseville, California, where we live to this day.

By watching retired people, I learned a few lessons worth noting. I decided we should not build a house much larger than 2000 square feet because I knew Ramona did not realize that she would someday not have the strength and energy she had at 30 but would still insist on keeping whatever size house we chose to live in antiseptically clean. Furthermore, any house with more than two bedrooms would turn her into a full-time motel owner and part-time maid.

Another lesson I had learned was that the stuff we thought our children would love to have after we died was, in general, a misconception. In other words, what one generation thinks is wonderful and valuable is a bit passé and impractical to the next. Furthermore, their own houses are usually completely furnished and full. As an example, one of our faculty members told me she had rented a storage bin over 20 years before in another state full of her "wonderful and valuable" belongings and was still paying the rent. She told me she thinks most of the contents are probably ruined. Hearing that, I determined we would not be renting a storage bin when we moved to California which meant we would give all of our excess possessions to the college or sell the rest. Even after divesting ourselves of a "ton" of stuff we had enough to fill a large moving van to furnish our new home. I also learned it was a long way to drive from the Boston area to California. It took us five days driving two cars.

My retirement years have proven to be very rewarding. We are surrounded with family and friends. Our daughter and son-in-law, Rachel and Bob Silva, and their three sons live just a few miles from us. We get together often, and they are our taxi service to and from the airport which is often.

We attend a wonderful church called Destiny in Rocklin. The pastor, Greg Fairrington who served as one of my interns when I was pastoring Bethel, founded the church in 1989; and it has grown to around 3,000 in average attendance. He and his wife, Kathy, are leading the congregation with anointed preaching and teaching. He is an exceptional preacher, and she often gives powerful exhortations. They have instituted what is called "The Wall," a monthly prayer meeting with attendance reaching up to 900. It is one of the healthiest Pentecostal churches I have ever seen. It does not hurt us a bit to watch our grandson Rylie Silva, one of the pastors, leading the young adults numbering well over 100 in average attendance. He has become such an excellent preacher that he fills in for the pastor in the three Sunday morning services from time to time.

Destiny Church is a prime example of what a twenty-first century Pentecostal church should look like. When the pastor, Greg Fairrington, founded the church, he was greatly influenced at the time by the popular "seeker-sensitive" movement. He was told by some of their leading "gurus" that if you were going to have a successful church plant in this modern culture, you must not be openly Pentecostal which means you should not allow any speaking in tongues and interpretation in the "main" services. If you believe Pentecostalism is biblical, be very careful to teach it only in small group settings or membership classes.

One of the leaders of the "seeker-sensitive" movement told Pastor Fairrington not to preach sermons on the blood of Jesus because it might scare new people away. For almost 20 years he followed their advice, and Destiny Church was known as a "seeker-sensitive" church. Pastor Fairrington will tell you that although the church grew numerically and financially, he became dissatisfied with the lack of spiritual growth. He began to pray and believe for the miraculous in the "main services." God answered his prayer, and now Destiny is a powerful, Christ-centered, and thoroughly Pentecostal church. I have heard the pastor preach some of the greatest sermons on the blood I have ever heard. Altar calls are given, and people are genuinely saved and miraculously healed. I have heard Greg at "The Wall" urge everyone to pray in their heavenly language and then lead them himself by praying in tongues over the microphone. All this tells me that if you want to build a powerful church in the twenty-first century, you must preach the whole Bible, including the blood of Christ, and hunger for the fruit and gifts of the Holy Spirit. It will take more than "church as usual" to confront the deception and evil the ordinary believer faces today and to have a positive impact on the culture.

Destiny Church has become very influential in the city by regularly sending teams of people to go into the public schools to refurbish and paint classrooms and do spring cleaning both inside and outside the schools. For ten years the church has provided the community a great Fourth of July celebration with an attendance of between 20,000-25,000 in one of the parks. It is a special treat for Ramona and me to watch Kent Ferrin, the son of Paul who was our music director at Bethel for ten years, coordinating the celebration and leading the choir for the event. In addition to Kent, about 50 of the people we pastored in San Jose attend Destiny.

Ramona meets with a group of seven retired ministers' wives to celebrate their birthdays, and I meet with six retired ministers once a month to study a portion of scripture and pray. It is a most enriching time. I often think how blessed we are not only to have close relationships with our family but also to have the joy of maintaining enduring friendships with our ministerial family from the past.

We travel a lot. I have come to the place where I would rather drive than fly so we put an inordinate number of miles on our vehicles. We drive from time to time to Colorado to see the Roncone family which includes our youngest daughter Rhonda and her husband Gene who pastor the great Highpoint Church in Aurora. It is a real pleasure to watch their three daughters and their husbands, all active and participating on the worship team. Morgan's husband, Caleb McNaughton, has become the senior associate pastor and is a wonderful preacher in his own right. It is worth the 900-mile drive from California to see four of our great grandchildren running and crawling in the lobby after a morning service and being loved by the church family.

Our trips to Colorado are tinged with sorrow because one of the Roncone family is missing. About three years into our retirement, we received the news that Geno, our 23-year-old grandson who had become an outstanding preacher and was on staff at the church in Aurora, was in the hospital. In less than eight hours, we were on the road to see him. It would be a seven-month long battle fighting a terribly rare form of cancer that would take him from us. I know that all grandparents are proud of their grandchildren, but Geno was very special. We had the joy of having him for two years at Northpoint Bible College studying for the ministry before the church board in Aurora asked if he would continue his studies in Denver and serve as the youth pastor because he had been so successful in building up the Youth Department when he was at home serving as a volunteer staff member. He was not only a very effective communicator but also a brilliant artist.

There were several things about Geno's life and death I will never understand. He told me on a couple of occasions that he would not live beyond the age of 40. He thought he might die in a car accident. During his illness, he fell in love with a beautiful young lady whom I know he would have married. When he died, she grieved like a widow. God gave Ramona and me a very special time with both of them. For some strange reason, Geno insisted that he and his girlfriend take us to lunch and that he would pay for it (grandparents ALWAYS pay!). Those two hours will live with us forever. We laughed and talked like four old friends. Near the end of his life, he told his dad he wanted to preach a special message God had given him. Of course, we jumped in the car again to hear him. He preached about Israel crossing the Red Sea. It was as if he were preaching to himself. He spoke of Israel surrounded by enemies not knowing if they would enter the promised land at that time, but God was with them. He told the congregation he did not know if it was time for him to cross over now or later. It turned out he crossed over a few weeks later. When he died, his nurses lined the hallway crying because they loved him so much. His main doctor, a brilliant Jewish woman, hugged my daughter and wept saying, "I'm so sorry; I have failed." In turn, Rhonda comforted her; and to this day they have a beautiful relationship. I believe God is going to use Geno's death to bring spiritual life and healing to that doctor, her family, and many others. I know I still will never understand why Geno was taken from us. In the natural, it is not supposed to be. I am reminded of the old Chinese proverb that says "Happiness is: grandfather dies, son dies, grandson dies." All I know is when Geno died, God set a beautiful rainbow outside his hospital window to comfort the family and tell us "in spite of the loss, all is well." His funeral drew hundreds of people to the church where he preached his last sermon, and the city sent a dozen police personnel to assist in parking and security at no cost. I still think of him every day.

In addition to driving to Colorado from time to time, we drive to Nashville to celebrate special days to be with our delightful daughter Renee, who works for American Airlines, and her children.

We have driven to Florida for General Councils and on one occasion drove from there to Greensboro, North Carolina, to preach for my nephew, David B. Crabtree, who has pastored Calvary Church for many years. In addition to pastoring, he serves as the assistant superintendent of the North Carolina District.

One of our more memorable trips in recent years was when we invited my sister, Charlotte, and her husband, Dr. Ray Carlson, to take a road trip to Nashville with us to visit their son Seth, who is excelling in the music business, and his family while we visited Renee and her family.

For many years Charlotte and I lived far apart and rarely had the chance to visit. I left home when she was only seven years old to attend CBI. In my estimation, Charlotte has the finest brain in the Crabtree clan. She was always an excellent student, got her degrees and teaching credentials, and to this day is a leader in the home schooling movement teaching over 80 students in her home in Redding, California. It is a personal pleasure to be able to see her more often. To add to her brain power, she met and married Ray, a clinical psychologist, who in my estimation is a genius. Mention any subject, and he can tell you a lot more than you want to know about it.

However, he is not a genius in driving. On the trip to Nashville, Ramona became very nervous when he drove our car. He would be driving 80 miles an hour guiding the steering wheel with two fingers and become so absorbed in a subject he was talking about that he would lose track of his speed and lose concentration on the traffic around him.

We obviously have to fly to Hawaii where we spend a month each year at our time-share, and quite often we have to fly to minister on Sundays or for three- or four-day conferences. Ramona almost always travels with me and still amazes people with her piano playing.

To sum it all up, Ramona and I have had a "great run" and ask God every day during devotions to bless our family and friends but, most importantly, to take each day we have left and let Him live through us.

For all my ministry I have enjoyed setting goals and celebrated when I met them. When I knew I was going to retire, I set what will probably be one of my final goals. I decided I wanted to be the happiest, most fulfilled retired Pentecostal preacher since the Book of Acts. I had observed and talked to so many retirees, including ministers, who had chosen to be unhappy, resentful, miserable, self-centered, angry, grouchy, disappointed, bitter, negative, and stingy and were always working hard to influence others to feel the same way. I decided I did not want any part of it so I decided to learn how not to retire. I believe I have uncovered a few secrets that will help me reach my goal.

A lot of people say they want to retire but still want both the perceived benefits of retirement and maintain the relationships and fulfillment of their former employment or ministry. Life, including retirement, is a tradeoff; and many people choose to be miserable when they are given the privilege to retire or, in some cases, forced to retire. Of course, there are many people who are unhappy with any major change in their lives. I will never forget the family who moved from Wisconsin to Iowa because of a new opportunity and promotion in the husband's profession.

They became faithful attendees at First Assembly. He seemed to be quite happy and settled, but she let me know how much better it was to live in Wisconsin. People were friendlier, they kept their houses better, the landscape was more beautiful, and the rivers and streams were crystal clear. She even believed the climate was better. Finally, I went to her husband and asked him if they were thinking of moving back to Wisconsin. He seemed quite shocked at the idea and said, "Oh, no pastor, we love it here in Des Moines." The next time I had a chance to talk to her, I called her by name and said words to the affect, "Your husband seems to be happy living in Iowa. I think it is time for you to stop trying to live in Wisconsin and decide to go ahead and enjoy living here." It seemed to help her because she never mentioned Wisconsin to me again. To be honest, when I finally visited Wisconsin, I had to admit that, overall, it was more beautiful than Iowa; but that fact did not make me unhappy living in Iowa.

Of course, change is not always comfortable, but it is foolhardy not to accept the inevitable and accept reality. I remember asking a pastor in his 70s why he did not retire. He told me that he knew a lot of preachers who had resigned from their churches and then were always looking for a place to preach. He told me it did not make any sense for him to go looking for a place to preach when he already had one. Good for him. I do hope he knew his preaching career is coming to an end in the next few years one way or another and will choose to accept the inevitable with a sense of fulfillment and contentment. I am honestly surprised at the age of 80 how often I am asked to preach. I will admit that I have not been asked to preach a youth convention for quite a while. I seem to be preaching more and more senior retreats and other events. However, I have made the decision with deep conviction that if I am never invited to preach again, I will accept it as the will of God and go on enjoying life.

It is important to embrace change by focusing on what you have and not on what you have lost by counting current blessings and discounting yesterday's failures and disappointments. After all, the gospel is good news for the past, present, and future. If the Lord is willing to forgive our past and cast our sins in the sea of His forgetfulness never to be remembered against us, we should be filled with gratitude for who we are in Him and what we have been given through His grace. I think it is all right to "humbly brag" about how good God has been to us. I have been to over 40 countries, and I would not trade America with all her problems for any other place to live. I have a wonderful wife, family, and friends. I have good health. I own a nice house with two cars in the garage. I have a good church to attend. I have all these things and heaven too. It would be a sin to choose to be unhappy and ungrateful.

It is important to embrace change and especially retirement by facing the inevitable by doing all you can do to make the transition from earth to heaven as easy as possible for everyone, especially your family. I have had a well-written will for many years for obvious reasons. Even if you do not have much to leave as an inheritance, you may meet an untimely death through the fault of others and your family could be awarded a large settlement that, without a will, be squandered by legal fees and unnecessary taxes and bypass those to whom you would want to have as beneficiaries including some family members, your church, or missions. It is also inevitable that your family will have to bear the cost of funeral expenses if you choose not to do so before you die. Ramona and I decided to pay for all our funeral expenses soon after we retired with the motivation to make it as easy as possible financially and otherwise on our family. Some people think all of this is morbid; I think all of this is wisdom. I believe the rapture taking place before I die is a real possibility in which case the anti-Christ is welcome to my casket and burial plot; however, if I die before the rapture, I want my family to have all my temporary money and stuff for their temporary use. Since the law allows me to make these arrangements, I would feel remiss if I were not a good steward of what the Lord has given me.

The second secret to a successful retirement is to choose to enjoy relationships with family and friends. I believe another word for life is relationships. Without them, life means simply a barren existence. As I write this, Ramona and I are grieving over a friend who has chosen to cut herself off from people who love her. Because the definition of death is separation, she is dead while she is physically alive.

If your spouse is still alive, choose to enjoy your relationship and not take it for granted. Ramona and I have a great time together even in our advanced years. We enjoy doing almost everything together including devotions, going to church, traveling, visiting family and friends, playing dominos and three to thirteen, cooking at home, going to restaurants on the spur of the moment, etc., etc.

Of course, it is important to remember there is a responsibility on our part to have and keep friends. The Bible speaks to the fact that if we are to have friends, we must in turn show ourselves friendly. As a pastor, I learned I needed best friends or intimate friends. These are people you have learned to trust to the point you not only enjoy being with them but also feel free to talk and pray through personal problems, knowing they will never break a confidence. I believe everyone needs best friends. I was shocked some time ago to hear a school psychologist recommending students be taught not to have best friends because the very term suggests discrimination and exclusion. In other words, if you have a best friend, it might make other students feel badly about themselves. There are some people who are educated beyond common sense to non-sense.

It is important not only to have best friends but also to have a lot of good friends. These are the people you enjoy getting together with if they live in close proximity for the purpose of fellowship. I have some friends who live a long distance from me, but we keep in touch from time to time. These are the people I may not have seen for months; but when we do get together, we pick up our conversation as if we had never been apart.

With all relationships, whether close friends or good friends or neighbors or business acquaintances, it is important never to tear down bridges unnecessarily but to keep them in good repair because it is amazing how both people and situations can change.

The third and most important secret to a successful retirement is to enrich your thought life in terms of the soul through prayer, meditation, and reading God's Word. The Bible is very clear that the thoughts you take to heart determine who you really are. The reason so many retirees are unhappy is because they are not comfortable being alone. They have little or no spiritual appetite so they are dependent on external stimuli and people for pleasure. They do everything in their power to avoid dealing with themselves in the light of eternity.

The Christian understands that the internal and eternal are far more important than the external and the temporary. Jesus spoke to these facts with a powerful illustration by using the story of a rich man found in Luke 12:16-21. The Living Bible is very graphic in its language:

16A rich man had a fertile farm that produced fine crops. 17In fact, his barns were full to overflowing—he couldn't get everything in. He thought about his problem, 18and finally exclaimed, "I know—I'll tear down my barns and build bigger ones! Then I'll have room enough. 19And I'll sit back and say to myself, 'Friend, you have enough stored away for years to come. Now take it easy! Wine, women, and song for you!'" 20But God said to him, "Fool! Tonight you die. Then who will get it all?" 21Yes, every man is a fool who gets rich on earth but not in heaven.

This account has had a profound effect on me as I have gotten older. I do not want to be a fool or fool myself. Death is inevitable and eternity is sure, but I can enrich my quality of life in heaven by being intentional in what I think and in what I do with the days I have left. Even a cup of cold water given in the right spirit and in the name of the Lord will have an eternal reward.

Death is not the end of my story, but I have enjoyed the few minutes I have had on this earth.

I have met a lot of interesting people, gone nearly around the world, and have few regrets; but the best is yet to come. Thank you for allowing me to share a few seconds of my temporary journey with you. I will talk to you later when time will not be an issue.

CPSIA information can be obtained
at www.ICGtesting.com
Printed in the USA
FSHW011557080119